Published by

Rick Baker

Ken Miller

Design and Layout
Ken Miller

Contributors
Simon Pritchard, William Martell, Russell Fox, David Gregory, Rick Baker, Johnny Burnett, Hector Martinez, Zilla Man

Special Thanks to
Gibran Evans, Jim Evans, David Gregory, Hector Martinez

Printing
IngramSpark

All rights reserved. No part of this publication may be reproduced or transmitted by any means, graphic, electronic or mechanical, including photocopying, recording, taping or any information storage and retrieval system, without prior written permission of the publishers. Copyright Eastern Heroes.

All photos & pictures © the copyright owners.

EASTERN HEROES FILM FRENZY

Issue 2 of *Eastern Heroes Film Frenzy* is here, and I really, really enjoyed putting this baby together!

2024 is the 70th anniversary of the release of the first Godzilla film, which gives me the excuse (as if I needed one) to include a large, 16-page Godzilla retrospective, looking back at all of the regal reptile's many movies. This year will also see the release of Severin Films' Bruceploitation boxset, which includes David Gregory's awesome documentary *Enter the Clones of Bruce*. So it only makes sense to pay homage to this upcoming release with a few pages crammed with colourful posters and some quotes from the actors who starred in these wild & wacky movies: Bruce Li, Bruce Le, Dragon Lee and Bruce Liang!

The gory, uber-cult samurai flick *Shogun Assassin*, which tells the story of swordsman-supreme Ogami Ittō and his son Daigorō, is undoubtedly the main theme of this issue. It has deservedly been made the centre of a multi-page, adoring celebration, which includes: a feature on the superb *Lone Wolf and Cub* manga, an astoundingly top-notch, all-new *Shogun Assassin* illustration by Russell Fox, a quick lowdown on all the movies that are associated with *Lone Wolf and Cub*, and much more! *Film Frenzy* has been very fortunate to get to speak with two key figures linked with the making of this movie: Jim Evans, who painted the movie poster and played an important part in bringing *Shogun Assassin* to the screen, and Gibran Evans, who supplied the very distinctive voice of little Daigorō. What I think is extra-cool is the fact that Jim and Gibran, who are so intrinsically linked to *Shogun Assassin*'s tale of a closely-bonded father and son duo, are, in fact, father and son themselves!

There's a whole bunch of Asian horror, sci-fi, cult, and fantasy films reviewed in this issue too, plus write-ups on another batch of mainland Chinese creature features, all of which have been written by me, just like in the first issue, but I've also snagged two guest reviewers this time around: author and screenwriter William Martell shares his thoughts on the stupendous kaiju movie *Godzilla Minus One*, and the successful book & magazine publisher Rick Baker (yes, him!) gives us the lowdown on the very entertaining *Enter the Clones of Bruce* documentary.

So what are you waiting for? You'd better start reading now!

Ken Miller
Editor

Shogun Assassin Illustrations
by Russell Fox

Godzilla Illustrations
by Zilla Man

Shogun Assassin is a production that defied all the odds: as a dubbed, re-edited flick that was created by splicing together the footage from two Japanese samurai movies, it was a film that should by all rights have entered the world as a fun, throwaway movie mongrel. And yet it transcended its lowly origins to become a much-loved, gore-drenched, pacy, very memorable, cult concoction!
As I've already mentioned, to pay tribute to this sword-swinging, arty, blood-spattered classic, *Film Frenzy* issue 2 is a *Shogun Assassin* special edition! Woot!

Okay, so the reason I've included the b&w version of comic book illustrator Russell Fox's amazing *Shogun Assassin* cover artwork here is because I want to talk about it! I believe that this drawing brilliantly encompasses both the vibes of the movie AND its manga origins.

I think it's really cool that this picture, drawn by an actual comic book artist, is quite obviously harking back to the *Lone Wolf and Cub* manga, which was the source material for the *Lone Wolf and Cub* movie series, which, in turn, was the source material for the Americanised *Shogun Assassin* film. But, at the same time, this illustration is depicting the lead characters of Ogami Ittō and young Daigorō as the movie actors Tomisaburo Wakayama and Tomikawa Akihiro, rather than portraying the father and child as they looked in the black and white pages of the original manga. The same goes for the wild-haired villain Retsudo/Shogun, who is drawn here to resemble actor Yūnosuke Itō.

Splendid stuff!

CONTENTS

06 - GODZILLA MINUS ONE - GUEST REVIEW
Scriptwriting guru **William Martell**'s verdict on the new Big G movie.

08 - SHOGUN ASSASSIN - A CELEBRATION - PART 1
All the cool *Shogun Assassin* features start here!

09 - THERE WILL BE BLOOD
An overview of the superb, gory samurai flick *Shogun Assassin*.

13 - ALL THE LONE WOLF AND CUB MOVIES
A quick lowdown on every *Lone Wolf and Cub* movie and TV show!

14 - MAGNIFICENT MANGA
Find out why the *Lone Wolf and Cub* comic is astoundingly good.

20 - BRUCEPLOITATION
David Gregory shares posters and quotes from the genre's top stars.

24 - GODZILLA - KING OF THE KAIJU
An appreciation of the city-stomping behemoth's many, many movies.

40 - FILM FRENZY REVIEWS
Reviews of Asian sci-fi, horror, fantasy and cult flicks!

48 - SHOGUN ASSASSIN - A CELEBRATION - PART 2
The *Shogun Assassin* celebration continues here!

49 - VOICE OF THE WOLF CUB
Gibran Evans, who gave Daigorō his voice in *Shogun Assassin*, talks to us!

58 - MASTER OF POSTERS
An interview with **Jim Evans**, painter of the iconic *Shogun Assassin* poster!

72 - LIGHTNING DISCS OF DEATH
Johnny Burnett tells us which *Shogun Assassin* Blu-rays & DVDs are the best!

76 - FANTABULOUS MEMORABILIA
Hector Martinez shows us his epic *Shogun Assassin* collection! Tasty stuff!

82 - BEASTS FROM THE EAST
Reviews of Chinese creature features: watch out for the teeth and tentacles!

90 - GIANT MONSTERS POSTER GALLERY
Feast your eyes on these stunning **Noriyoshi Ohrai** artworks.

106 - ENTER THE CLONES OF BRUCE - GUEST REVIEW
Eastern Heroes head honcho **Rick Baker** fills us in on this documentary.

THE MONSTER ZONE BLOG

GREAT APES!

MEGA REPTILES!

BULL MEN!

Devoted to every kind of movie and TV monster, from King Kong to Godzilla, from alien blobs to the bull men in *A Chinese Odyssey Part Two*, plus fantastic beasts from other media, including books, posters and comics. The Monster Zone Blog, curated by Ken Miller, the author of *The New Essential Guide to Hong Kong Movies* and the editor of *Film Frenzy* magazine, features many Asian creature feature reviews amongst the seething mass of international monster movie write-ups that lurk on the blog site!

https://monsterzone.org

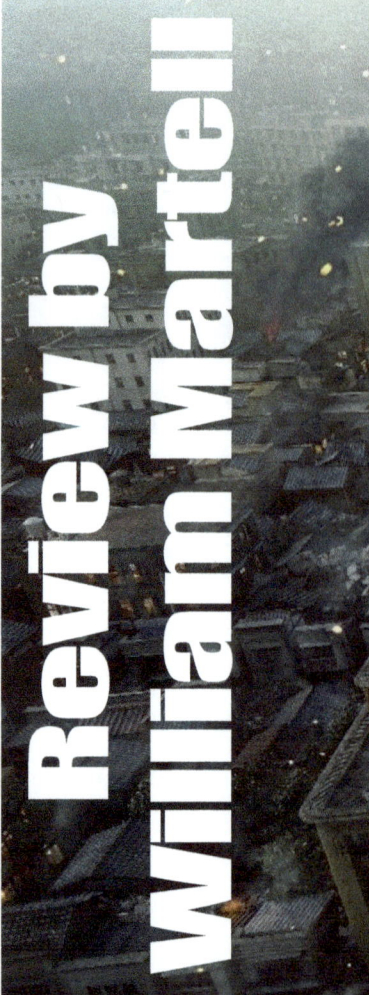

Review by William Martell

GODZILLA MINUS ONE (2023)

*Starring Minami Hamabe, Ryunosuke Kamiki, Sakura Ando, Kuranosuke Sasaki, Munetaka Aoki
Written by Takashi Yamazaki
Directed by Takashi Yamazaki
Toho Studios*

Godzilla Minus One proves that you can make a serious movie with big emotional moments... that also works as popcorn entertainment. Yes, this is a Godzilla movie. But it's also about the trauma of war, feelings of failure and responsibility for the deaths of others, how people and families are displaced after war, and living with the horrors of war haunting every moment of your life. And Godzilla.

It's also an exciting film, and the director has obviously seen *Jaws* (1975) because we get several scenes that were inspired by that film - including barrels sinking below the surface and the fin chasing the ship. All of this might not be obvious to the

casual viewer, however, because it's used in different ways.

This film makes you care deeply about characters... and then Godzilla attacks. Some characters may not survive...

One of the great things about this film is how well it sets up all of the twists and turns of the plot. Also, how it gives us information visually that ramps up the suspense. When Godzilla is present under the water, the fish die and float to the surface. That happens in one of the first scenes... so that later on, on a boat when the dead fish start popping to the surface in the background, we know what this means.

Another nice set up involves Godzilla using his nuclear option: his "fins" grow and glow. So, when that happens, you really know that you're screwed. Godzilla can destroy anything!

This is exciting and emotional and probably the first Godzilla movie where I really cared about the characters, and you probably could have removed Godzilla and it could have still worked well as a drama film. But with Godzilla? More dramatic, more emotional, more exciting.

Hollywood - this is how it's done.

Shin Godzilla (2016), which was all about government bureaucracy in its response to a Godzilla attack, was both a Godzilla movie and a comedy or satire film about how government fails to solve problems because no one wants to be responsible if a plan fails. Both that film and *Godzilla Minus One* use Godzilla to look at real life issues.

We are in the Godzilla Renaissance!

SHOGUN ASSASSIN OVERVIEW

THERE WILL BE BLOOD

Ken Miller looks at what makes *Shogun Assassin* so bloody good...

Vivid, blood-spraying carnage, impeccable use of voice-overs, gorgeous cinematography, a fascinating feudal Japanese setting, a lethal wooden perambulator, and a thrilling electronic score written by Mark Lindsay (formerly of the band Paul Revere & the Raiders) and W. Michael Lewis (one-time keyboard player with the band Quicksilver Messenger Service), ensured that *Shogun Assassin* became a cult favourite after its grindhouse movie circuit release in the US (by New World Pictures), and then later when it was unleashed as a video cassette by Vipco in the UK and MCA/Universal Home Video in America.

Shogun Assassin would end up being included on the BBFC's banned list of films (the infamous 'Video Nasties' list) and the movie was prosecuted for obscenity, but the prosecution failed.

Like so many fans of *Shogun Assassin*, when I first viewed this movie during its initial video release I didn't know that it was, in fact, an Americanised concoction created by splicing footage from two different Japanese films together. These movies, *Lone Wolf and Cub: Sword of Vengeance* (1972) and *Lone Wolf and Cub: Baby Cart at the River Styx* (1972), were the first two of six films based on the popular manga series *Lone Wolf and Cub*, which told the story of the Shogun's lethal executioner, Ogami Ittō, becoming a ronin after the murder of his wife. Would I have thought differently about *Shogun Assassin* had I seen the original films first?

Perhaps I would have, but I don't think so, as this production somehow manages to go way beyond its potentially trashy cut-and-paste origins to become a unique, bloody cool and memorable movie thanks to its own very special qualities, namely the effective use of dubbing, the reworked, tight plot and the damn catchy, driving synth soundtrack.

Robert Houston, who'd acted in *The Hills Have Eyes* (1977) and *1941* (1979), became a first-time director, producer and writer with *Shogun Assassin*, a project that came into being with the help of co-writer and co-producer David Weisman, who'd been a movie poster designer, an assistant to Otto Preminger, and had co-written, co-produced and co-directed cult flick *Ciao Manhattan* (1972). Weisman would go on to be instrumental in the financing and making

of the Oscar-winning *Kiss of the Spider Woman* (1985), and was the art director and title designer for the nihilistic, mondo-style cult doc *The Killing of America* (1981). Another collaborator was movie & rock poster artist/designer Jim Evans, who not only was the person who urged the late David Weisman to buy the rights to the *Lone Wolf and Cub* movies, he also created the legendary *Shogun Assassin* poster and was the father of Gibran Evans, the boy who provides the voice of Ogami Ittō's son Daigorō!

I'm pretty sure even Robert Houston himself, who made Academy award-winning documentary *Mighty Times: The Children's March* (2004), would be the first to acknowledge that being referred to as the 'director' of Shogun Assassin is quite a stretch! All the wonderful direction is obviously courtesy of Kenji Misumi, the Japanese director of the two source movies. Misumi directed two of the other Lone Wolf and Cub movies as well: 1972's *Lone Wolf and Cub: Baby Cart to Hades* and 1973's *Lone Wolf and Cub: Baby Cart in the Land of Demons* (1972's *Lone Wolf and Cub: Baby Cart in Peril* was directed by Buichi Saitō and 1974's *Lone Wolf and Cub: White Heaven in Hell* was directed by Yoshiyuki Kuroda).

Suffice to say, Kenji Misumi (who also directed 1972's *Hanzo the Razor: Sword of Justice*, which was another film based on a manga written by Kazuo Koike, the writer of the *Lone Wolf and Cub* manga) deserves all of the praise when it comes to *Shogun Assassin*'s visual panache. Widescreen wonderfulness abounds throughout!

Beautiful cinematography and brutality rub shoulders, most strikingly when slo-mo jets of blood spurt from the neck of a decapitated adversary standing in a gorgeous-looking, sun-bathed field!

The gory aspects of *Shogun Assassin* certainly stick in the memory. Some of the vicious, bloodstained moments include: a sword getting wedged in an attacker's forehead, a ninja losing ears, fingers and other body parts as he attempts to escape from a room full of female assassins, a head being hacked completely in two by Ittō's blade, and throats and chests erupting with super-charged geysers of blood!

These action scenes can border on the outlandish, as assailants disguised a peasant women hurl vegetables with knives

Beautiful and brutal images unite in this shot...

Ogami Ittō fights female assassins who are dressed as travelling performers!

hidden inside them, the wooden baby cart sprouts shin-slicing blades from its wheels, and Ogami Ittō carries his son on his back, then bends over so that sunlight glints off a mirror attached to Daigorō's head to dazzle an opponent during a duel.

Other sequences are just a joy to watch, whether it's Ittō sitting in a bath, checking the room for danger, as the camera does a slow, wary 360-degree circle of the place, or the shots of little Daigorō doing his best to bring water from a river to give to his injured father, finally resorting to carrying the water to Ittō in his mouth.

An early scene, showing Ogami Ittō putting a sword and a ball in front of his very young son, in a test to see whether Daigorō chooses the toy (and hence will soon be joining his dead mother in heaven) or the blade (and will be accompanying his father on his road to vengeance), perfectly encapsulates the dour lead character's uncompromising mindset. As played by Tomisaburo Wakayama, Ittō is a stoic, imperturbable character who never backs down and always kills his enemies, with the exception of a senior female assassin whom Ittō shows mercy to after she hesitates in a face-off in which his son's life hangs in the balance. Wakayama, brother of actor Shintaro Katsu (the star of the *Zatoichi* blind swordsman movie series), is not your typical leading man. Unlike the more handsome, prime physical specimen depicted in the manga, Tomisaburo Wakayama is a stern, somewhat plain dude with, let's face it, a dad bod! Yet this somehow enhances Lone Wolf's scowling onscreen presence, as we watch this character, who is definitely no ripped, powerful-looking badass, overcome all the obstacles and adversaries in his path, simply because he's an implacable dude who is really, really good at what he does: fighting and killing!

Arresting images abound in *Shogun Assassin*, many relating to the Masters of Death, super-fighter bodyguards who wear roningasa hats (made from bamboo palms) and are armed with weapons specific to each character: a club, iron claws, spiked gloves. At one point, as the Masters of Death cross a desert landscape, we see the lead Master plunge his iron claws into the sand... and blood begins to seep to the surface. A very memorable visual! It's revealed that rebels are hiding beneath the desert sands and the Masters of Death soon begin bloodily dealing with them, but Ogami Ittō is also waiting in the dunes... and the Masters of Death finally get a violent taste of their own medicine.

All of this impressive imagery is courtesy of the source material, of course. Around

Blood and sand

12 minutes from the first *Lone Wolf and Cub* movie and the rest of the footage taken from the second in the series. But it's how it's all mixed into this newly edited and dubbed brew that imbues *Shogun Assassin* with its own individual flavour.

First and foremost, the new English dub works wonderfully, especially the matter-of-fact/innocent tones of Daigorō, delightfully voiced by Gibran Evans, who, sounding like a genuine young boy (which he was at the time), acts as the narrator of the story. This use of voice-over allows Houston and Weisman to alter the narrative, streamlining the tale, discarding the story thread (from the manga and original films) involving the Yagyū clan, turning the clan's leader, Retsudo, into the crazed Shogun in this self-contained plot. In the reworked script Daigorō tells us that the Shogun has gone mad, "People said his brain was infected by devils." The child's voice goes on to explain why Ogami Ittō becomes a ronin, "Then, one night, the Shogun sent his ninja spies to our house. They were supposed to kill my father, but they didn't. That was the night everything changed, forever. That was when my father left his samurai life and became a demon. He became an assassin who walks the road of vengeance. And he took me with him." Wonderful stuff!

Quotable dialogue abounds in the film, such as when the Masters of Death leader, with a fine spray of blood spritzing from his severed jugular vein, waxes lyrical about the nature of the wound Ittō has inflicted on him: "Your technique is magnificent. When cut across the neck, a sound like wailing winter winds is heard, they say. I'd always hoped to cut someone like that someday, to hear that sound. But to have it happen to my own neck is... ridiculous." Wow!

The reworking of the story condenses the plot, so that the fights, the face-offs, the confrontations and story beats occur in quick succession, really adding to the movie's pace.

The other key new element is, obviously, the cool, propulsive soundtrack, most of it performed on a Prophet-5 synthesizer. This score, recorded by Mark Lindsay and W. Michael Lewis over at Lindsay's Wonderland Avenue studio in the Los Angeles Hills, is definitely one of the big points of difference between *Shogun Assassin* and the Japanese *Lone Wolf and Cub* films.

The sound effects, as the weapons are zinged about, etc, were created at the Wonderland Avenue studio

ITALIAN POSTER FOR *LONE WOLF AND CUB: BABY CART AT THE RIVER STYX*
Footage from 1972's *Lone Wolf and Cub: Baby Cart at the River Styx* formed a large part of what became *Shogun Assassin*...

too, produced on an E-mu Modular System (a large, wall-sized synth) and recorded on a Trident Fleximix console.

Somehow a special alchemy occurred within all these elements, as the original footage was merged with the new dub, gelling together well, resulting in such a unique vibe that Shogun Assassin remains a very memorable chanbara (samurai film) that definitely continues to generate a nostalgic frisson for those viewers, including myself, who first saw this furiously good 'n' gory flick in their formative years.

Look, the movie is awesome, okay? Really awesome!

One of the Masters of Death gets skewered!

ALL THE LONE WOLF AND CUB MOVIES...

Ken Miller provides a quick lowdown on every Lone Wolf and Cub movie that has been produced so far, including, of course, Shogun Assassin, plus the television shows...

LONE WOLF AND CUB: SWORD OF VENGEANCE (1972)
Six Lone Wolf and Cub films starring Tomisaburo Wakayama as Ogami Ittō and Tomikawa Akihiro as Daigorō were made. The first movie focuses on Lone Wolf and Cub's origin, when Ogami Ittō, the Shogun's decapitator, is framed for treason by the Yagyū clan, resulting in Ittō hitting the vengeance trail with his son.

LONE WOLF AND CUB: BABY CART AT THE RIVER STYX (1972)
Ogami Ittō takes-on a group of female assassins in the employ of the Yagyū clan and must assassinate a traitor planning to sell his clan's secrets to the Shogunate, but this man is guarded by three lethal brothers... the Gods of Death.

LONE WOLF AND CUB: BABY CART TO HADES (1972)
The third film features a ronin who wants a duel with Ittō, a prostitute whom Ittō comes to the aid of, even allowing himself to be tortured, plus more assassins sent by the Yagyū clan and a battle with an army of adversaries.

LONE WOLF AND CUB: BABY CART IN PERIL (1972)
Here Ittō deals with a grudge-bearing swordsman called Gunbei and a topless, tattooed female killer called Oyuki, he vanquishes an entire army, and gets to cross swords with Yagyū leader Retsudo.

LONE WOLF AND CUB: BABY CART IN THE LAND OF DEMONS (1973)
Ittō duels with five different warriors of the Kuroda clan, each of whom delivers a portion of the information Itto requires to take on his latest contract. Meanwhile, Daigorō is caught up in a subplot involving a female pickpocket.

LONE WOLF AND CUB: WHITE HEAVEN IN HELL (1974)
Ittō faces off against hordes of clansmen led by the one-eyed Lord Retsudo. Horror elements are mixed into the narrative with the introduction of zombie warriors who can burrow through the ground. An icy encounter sees Ittō battle hordes of skiing enemies!

SHOGUN ASSASSIN (1980)
The cool, fun, rejigged, dubbed American release that uses footage from the first two Japanese Lone Wolf and Cub movies and retools the plot, turning the Retsudo character into the Shogun. The Gods of Death brothers from Baby Cart at the River Styx are renamed the Masters of Death here.

LONE WOLF AND CUB: FINAL CONFLICT (1993)
A revisionist reboot that changes Ogami Ittō's character (here played by Masakazu Tamura), turning him into a sensitive father who cries... which is far removed from the stoic Ogami Ittō seen in the first six movies. The story concentrates on Ittō's mission of revenge against the Yagyū clan, ignoring the assassin-for-hire subplots. Yushi Shoda plays Daigorō.

LONE WOLF AND CUB TV SERIES (1973-1976)
This show ran for three seasons. The episodes were 45 minutes long. It was originally aired on Nippon TV in Japan, and was broadcast in the US titled The Fugitive Samurai. Starring Kinnosuke Nakamura as Ogami Ittō and Kazutaka Nishikawa as Daigorō in the first two seasons, replaced by Takumi Satô as the son in the third season.

TV movies were aired in Japan in connection with the 70's television series. **KOZURE ÔKAMI: OSANAGO NO ME (1985)** and **KOZURE ÔKAMI: NAMIDA ITO (1986)** both starred the TV series actor Kinnosuke Nakamura as Ittō.

LONE WOLF AND CHILD: ASSASSIN ON THE ROAD TO HELL (1989)
This standalone 140 minute TV movie covers much of the Lone Wolf and Cub saga, starring Takahashi Hideki as Ittō, directed by Tanaka Tokuzo. TV production values and toned-down gore. Directed by Tokuzô Tanaka and written by Masahiro Shimura, with Tomisaburo Wakayama playing the villainous Retsudo!

LONE WOLF AND CUB TV SERIES (2002-2004)
Kin'ya Kitaôji plays Ogami Ittō in this series, with Tsubasa Kobayashi in the role of Daigorō, and Isao Natsuyagi playing Retsudo, in a show produced by TV Asahi and Toei Company.

MAGNIFICENT MANGA

A LOOK AT THE SUPERB COMIC THAT SPAWNED THE MOVIES

SHOGUN ASSASSIN ARTICLE

By Ken Miller

The manga series *Lone Wolf and Cub* (known as *Kozure Ōkami* in Japan), created by writer Kazuo Koike and artist Goseki Kojima, was first published in 1970 and chronicled the story of Ogami Ittō, the Shogun's executioner, who is disgraced and framed by the supremely cunning villain Yagyu Retsudo of the Yagyū clan, forcing Ittō to take the path of the assassin after his wife is murdered and he refuses to commit seppuku. Bringing along his son, Daigorō, Ittō seeks revenge on the Yagyū clan and must tackle the many foes sent to kill him, whilst also taking on assassin-for-hire jobs, which he only undertakes after his employers are totally honest with Ittō, keeping no secrets from him.

Lone Wolf and Cub was originally published in the US in a translated English edition by First Comics, back in 1987, but the company unfortunately went bankrupt before all of the issues could be published.

I started reading the stories in 2000, when Dark Horse Comics began releasing their *Lone Wolf and Cub* trade paperbacks, which were similar in design to the volumes published in Japan. All the stories were released in 28 volumes over a two-year period, with cover art supplied by top comic artists Frank Miller (with Lynn Varley),

Here is the scene in which Ogami Ittō waits for his son Daigorō to choose between a ball and a sword, a decision that will change the course of his son's life forever, as depicted in the manga and in the film *Lone Wolf and Cub: Sword of Vengeance* (1972), footage that was also used in *Shogun Assassin* (1980)...

Matt Wagner, Guy Davis (with Vince Locke) and Bill Sienkiewicz (some of these cover illustrations were originally created for the First Comics series). The Dark Horse editions came with a glossary at the back to explain many of the Edo-era terms used in the stories. Dark Horse would later rerelease all these stories in a set of 12 larger format omnibus editions.

Kazuo Koike's plotting in this manga series is flawless. Stories are structured with precision, balancing tons of Tokugawa shogunate-era world-building detail, deft characterisation, and expertly-handled twists and reveals wonderfully. When I read the first story, *Son for Hire, Sword for Hire*, I was immediately sucked into this harsh world of skilled swordsmen, action, the internecine strife within feudal clans, and the unorthodox central relationship between Ogami Ittō and his son Daigorō. But what really sealed the deal and made me a *Lone Wolf and Cub* manga fan was the cool, unexpected turnabout in this story: Koike throws in a great twist as we realise that the clan warriors who've used a special 'hawk-wing eye attack' technique to hunt down and capture Ittō have actually been tricked! Ittō <u>wanted</u> to be caught all along and had even written a fake warning message to the clan, telling them that he was an assassin travelling with a small child, thus guaranteeing that he'd get identified, arrested, and taken to the clan's castle... so that he could kill his targets! This sort of writing is a constant in the manga, ensuring the stories are never as straightforward as they sometimes might seem at the outset of each wonderfully-formed yarn. Along with the twists, the tales are also prone to keep readers guessing as to whom Ittō is actually going to kill, and the means by which Lone Wolf goes about his tasks in the plots can also be surprising.

Kioke populates the world of these stories with every kind of character: ronin, soldiers, peasants, thieves, samurai, lords, ladies, innkeepers, poisoners, priests, prostitutes, stage performers, elders, chieftains, monks, yakuza, riflemen, policemen, ninjas, crippled ninjas, archers, sleeper agents, and every other character-type to be found in Edo-period Japan. Some of these people are honourable, some are devious, some are pitiable, some are evil or murderous,

A cover illustration by Frank Miller and Lynn Varley

and others are degenerate grotesques. Kazuo Koike surrounds all these folks in a well-researched period milieu, working Japanese history into the narrative, whilst never allowing the detail to impede the flow of the plots, and his deft handling of the characters makes the bizarre and outlandish things that sometimes occur in the yarns seem believable.

The chapters are a mixture of standalone adventures and murder-for-hire missions, peppered with backstory flashbacks, and an overarching plot line involving Retsudo and his laser-focused need to take down Ittō. This story thread becomes more and more foregrounded as the series progresses. Towards the end of the saga, after a bounty is put on Ittō's head, pretty much the whole of Japan is gunning for him! But there's an ebb and flow to this grand tale too, and this is definitely part of its strength, because the stories aren't just nonstop tales of bloodbaths and killings: there are tales that are more intimate, there's character development, there's the critical look at the intricacies of feudal Japanese notions of honour and duty, and, of course, there's the central relationship between Lone Wolf and his Cub.

Perfectly complimenting Kioke's writing is the wondrous art of Goseki Kojima. His b&w illustrations exude an incredibly cinematic visual storytelling style, and I'm

The Hidari Brothers, also known as The Bentenrai Brothers, as they appear in the manga (above), and how they look (below) in the film *Lone Wolf and Cub: Baby Cart at the River Styx* (1972), where they are referred to as the Gods of Death. They look very similar to their manga counterparts! Footage of them is used in *Shogun Assassin* (1980) too, where they are called the Masters of Death…

In the *Lone Wolf and Cub* manga, the lead Hidari Brother uses his metal claws to pull rebels from beneath the sand. The same thing happens in the movie *Lone Wolf and Cub: Baby Cart at the River Styx* (1972) and, of course, in *Shogun Assassin* (1980)…

sure that many of these panels worked as readymade storyboards when the *Lone Wolf and Cub* movies were produced.

Kojima manages to infuse a sense of the 'fog of war' into his fight sequences, using multiple speed lines to turn some of the action panels into a blur of motion, making the reader unsure of quite what is happening during the fights! Conversely, exquisitely-composed establishing shots

Various characters wear distinctive headgear in the *Lone Wolf and Cub* manga series and also in the *Lone Wolf and Cub* movies...

Swords are drawn...

of temples, tree-shrouded trails, forested valleys and other scenic delights not only set the scene for the stories, they also demand that the reader should slow down a little and pay full attention to the detail.

The effective use of wide-angle panels, which spread across two pages, adds to the dynamism of sequences. Pages of compelling, dialogue-free sequential art keep you glued to the story, such as when the Yagyū clan marches through a rain-swept landscape, or when a group of unspeaking 'nighthawk' prostitutes approach a remote shack that Lone Wolf and Cub are sleeping in.

Yagyu Retsudo (above & left) as he is drawn in the *Lone Wolf and Cub* manga. This cunning, extremely ruthless and manipulative lead villain may have been an old man, but he was also a wily, tough fighter. In *Lone Wolf and Cub: Sword of Vengeance*, Yagyu Retsudo was played by Yūnosuke Itō (below). In the *Shogun Assassin* plot alterations his character was turned into the mad Shogun...

From the massive to the minuscule, panels with no figures in them are utilised to emanate a sense of mood and place, whether showing the close-up view of a stone road marker or the full page vista of a flock of birds flying across a cloudy dawn sky.

Kojima's art alternates between panels crammed with fine black line work, to others using greyscale washes, to panels that are a mixture of line work and areas of full black. All this b&w imagery makes Lone Wolf and Cub the distinctive manga classic that it is, and there's no doubt that adding colour to this artwork would ruin the special vibe of the saga.

Koike and Kojima's talents combined here to create one of the greatest ever examples of manga, which deserves all of the praise it has garnered over the years. It is a stunning tale that, through well-rendered words and pictures, exudes heaps of atmosphere, mixes meditations and violent action together, evokes a totally complete sense of place, and brings to life a plethora of memorable characters, especially the titular duo of father and son.

There was a follow-up manga series to Lone Wolf and Cub, called Shin Kozure Ookami - Lone Wolf, released in English as New Lone Wolf and Cub by Dark Horse Comics in 2014. It was written again by Kazuo Koike and drawn this time by Hideki Mori (Goseki Kojima had passed away in 2000). The 11 volume series focused on Daigorō and Tōgō Shigetada of the Satsuma clan, who is a skilled master of the Jigen-ryu sword style.

Dark Horse Comics also released Samurai Executioner, a manga written by Koike and drawn by Kojima, focusing on Yamada Asaemon, the man entrusted with testing the edge and quality of the Shogun's newly forged swords. Asaemon actually appears in the Lone Wolf and Cub crossover story Decapitator Asaemon, where he duels with Ogami Ittō. This tale is included in Black Wind, volume 5 of the Dark Horse Lone Wolf and Cub series.

If you're thinking of immersing yourself in this world for the first time, be sure to start with the original Lone Wolf and Cub series and plunge into an epic yarn that's full of compelling characters, dramatic fight scenes, and intriguing narratives, all of which is layered with a superbly evoked exploration of the customs, history, caste system, honorifics, and terminology of Edo-period Japan.

The Shogun Assassin Celebration continues on page 48

BRUCEPLOITATION

No Asian film genre is quite as cult as the Bruceploitation sub-genre!

After the untimely death of Bruce Lee, the world still wanted MORE Bruce Lee movies, so the Bruceploitation genre quickly developed. It's amazing to think that a genre existed that was entirely centred around a single actor, a single person: the late, great Bruce Lee!

Bruce Lee biopics, sequels to Bruce Lee movies, spin-offs and even insane horror & sci-fi-tinged movies shot into cinemas. They told (often very fictionalised) tales of Bruce Lee's life, or introduced brothers of characters Bruce played in his own films, or they had protagonists look into Bruce's demise, or the movies focused on fighters setting out to avenge Bruce's death. Some productions simply just tried to pass-off lookalike actors as the REAL Bruce Lee! German distributors were especially guilty of this practice, hoodwinking patrons into thinking these films featured footage of the actual Bruce Lee.

You name it, it probably happened in a Bruceploitation film: Bruce fighting Popeye and Dracula! Bruce's spirit appearing in a martial arts teacher's dream to urge him to investigate the circumstances surrounding his death! Bruce getting cloned and then teaming-up with other Bruces! Bruce fighting back from the grave!

Director **David Gregory** has captured this wonderful, weird and wild period perfectly in his new doc, Enter the Clones of Bruce, which has garnered many rave reviews during its screenings at film festivals around the world. To help celebrate the upcoming release of the documentary in a Severin Films Bruceploitation boxset, David has shared with us some fine poster images, plus quotes from Bruce Li, Bruce Le, Dragon Lee and Bruce Liang, who are the cool, legendary Bruceploitation actors that appear in David's film...

Bruce Li

Bruce Le

Dragon Lee

Bruce Liang

"I do like it because I wasn't acting as Bruce Lee, but as his little brother. I wasn't imitating him! I was myself."
BRUCE LI talking about *Fist of Fury 2*

"I owe my career to Bruce Lee because if he didn't exist then I wouldn't have been able to film movies and my career path would've been altered."
DRAGON LEE reflects on what he owes the real Bruce Lee

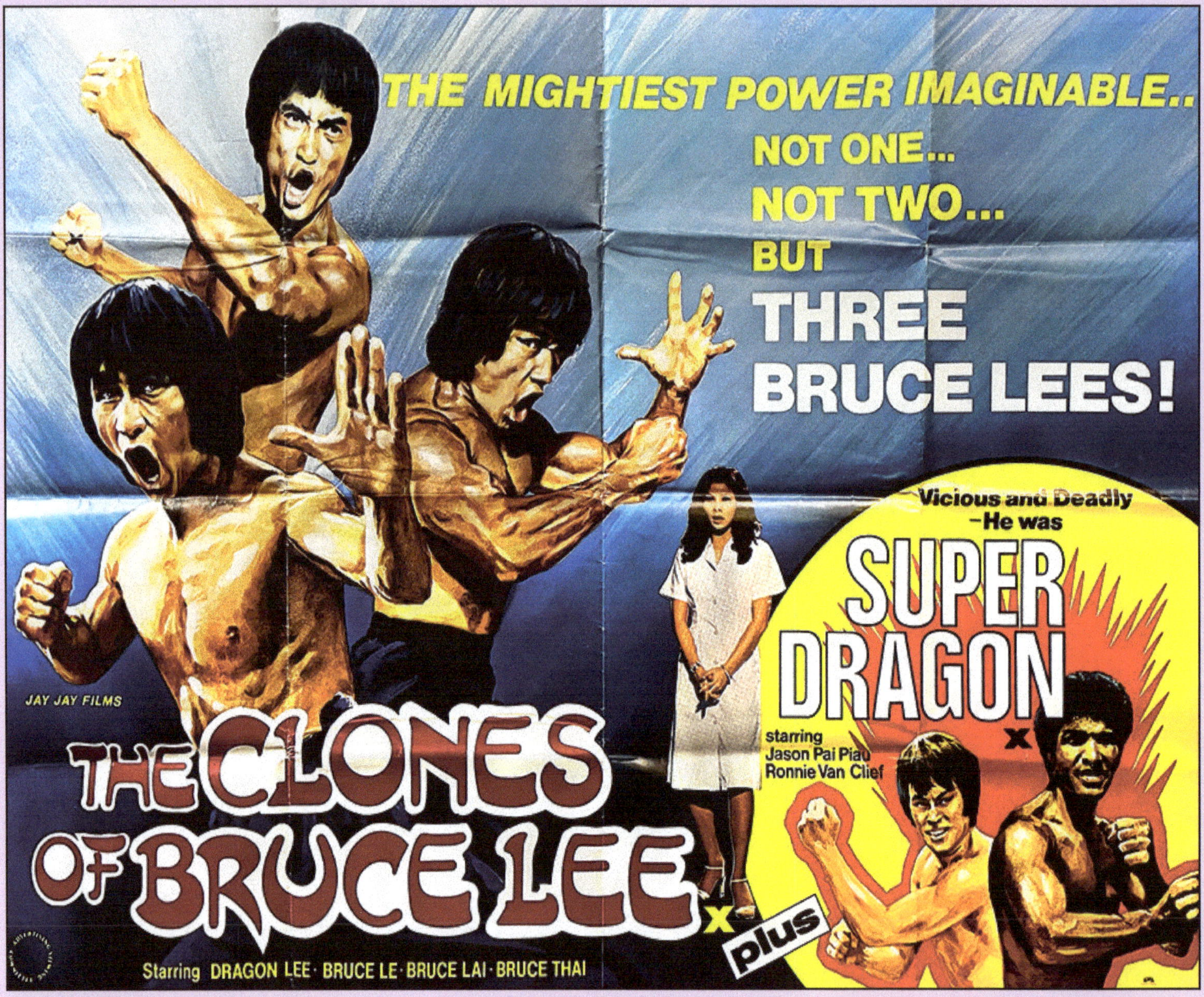

"In my movies, the kung fu moves are simple, but I strived to make them powerful and deadly. I hoped that audiences found them compelling."
BRUCE LE on keeping his martial arts moves straightforward but lethal

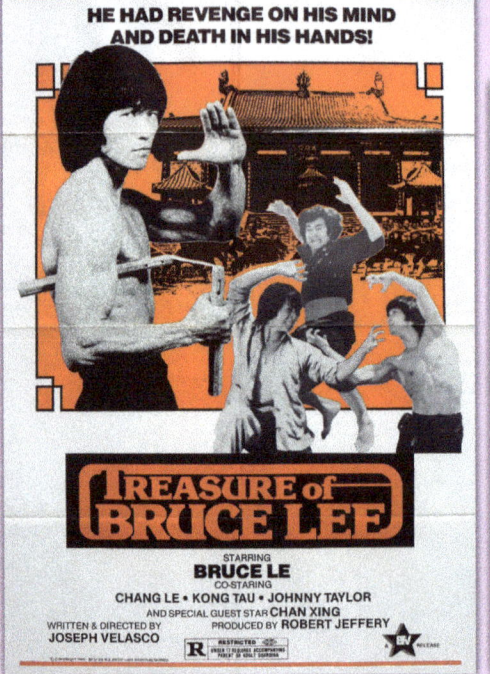

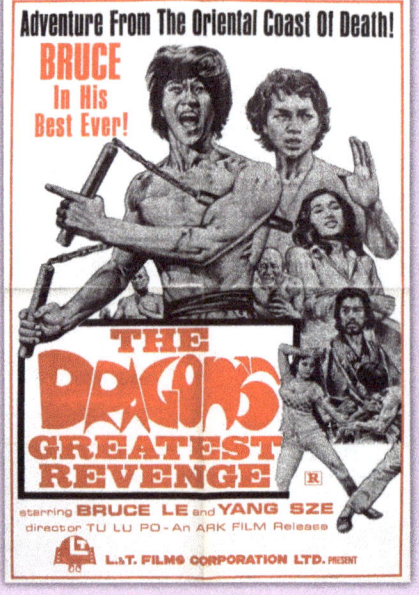

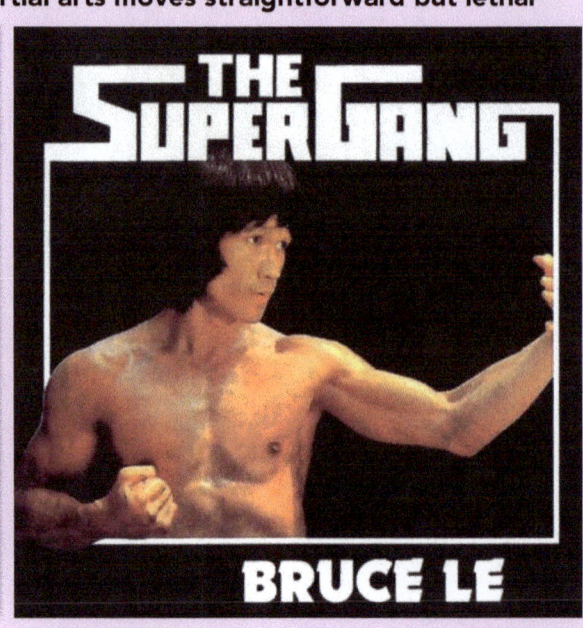

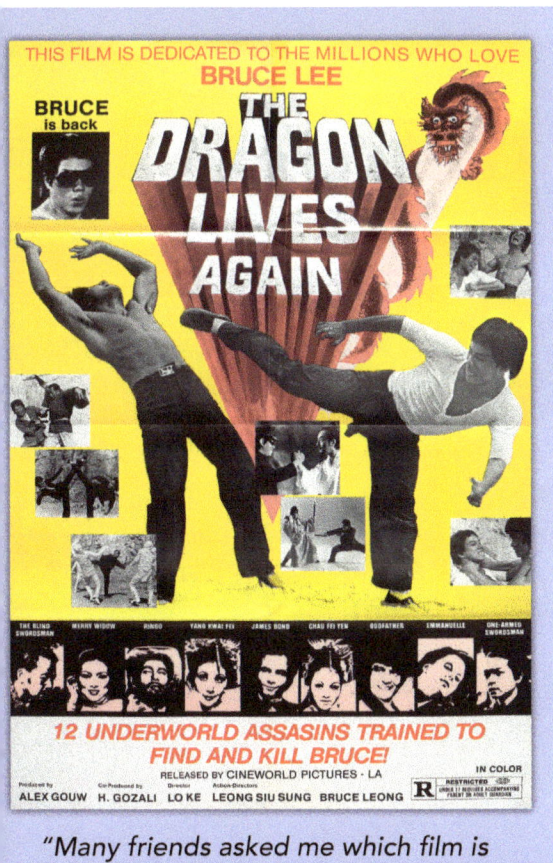

"Many friends asked me which film is my favourite? I can only say every film, because I put my heart into every single one."
BRUCE LIANG on why he likes all of his movies

The Dragon Lives Again!

"I didn't think I looked like Bruce Lee. I didn't think so. But I could imitate him because I studied him closely."
BRUCE LI on whether he resembled Bruce Lee

The tribute to the Bruceploitation sub-genre continues in THE CLONES OF BRUCE LEE SPECIAL EDITION, from *Eastern Heroes!* This publication will be crammed full of goodies, including a huge poster gallery section and an in-depth look at Severin's entertaining documentary *Enter the Clones of Bruce*, plus reviews of all the movies that are part of the upcoming Bruceploitation boxset from Severin Films!

HARDCOVER AND PAPERBACK VERSIONS WILL BE AVAILABLE IN MARCH!

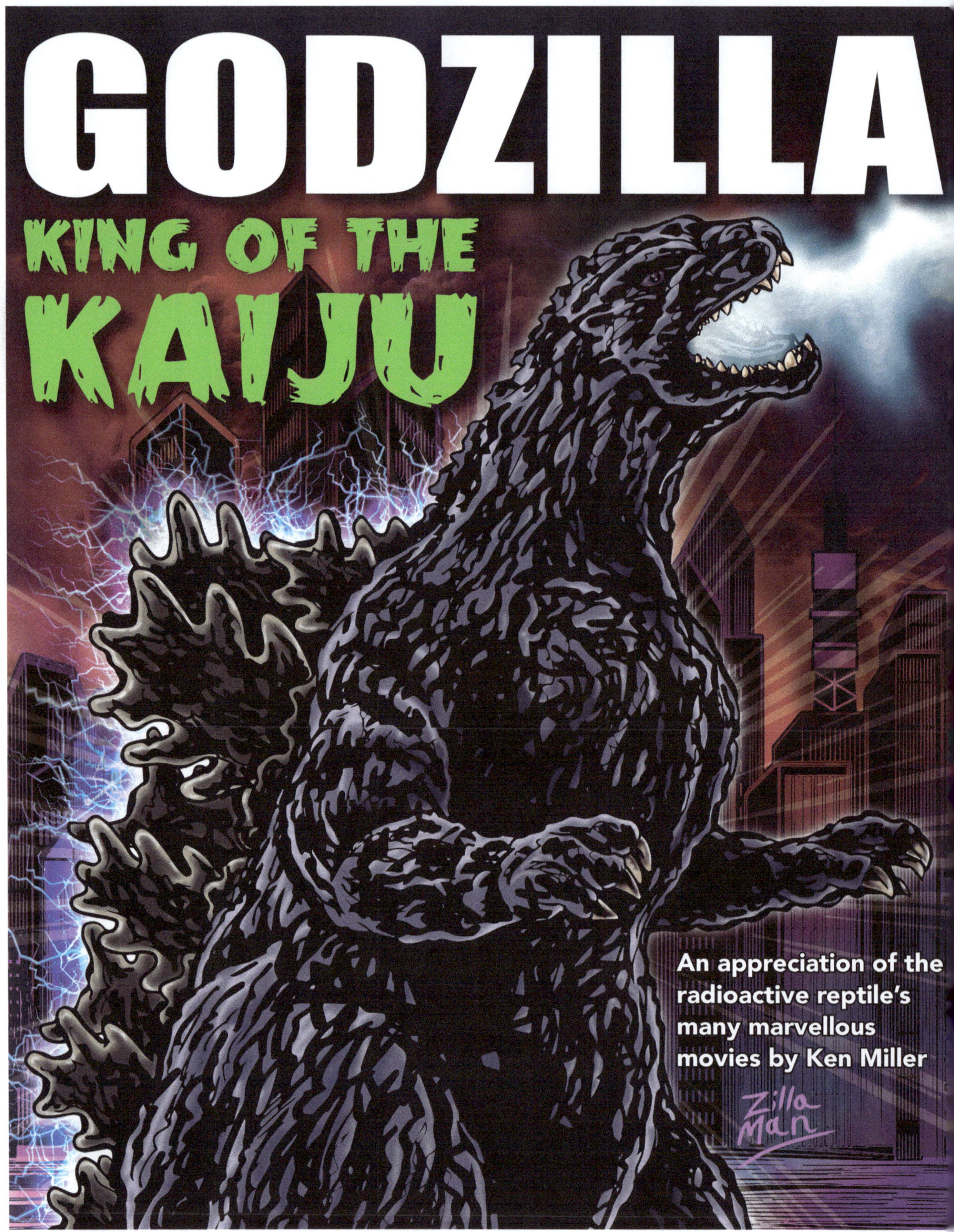

Godzilla, the big, roaring, reptilian star of so many giant monster movies, has repeatedly evolved over the decades. This gigantic super-beast has been depicted as a foe, as an anti-hero, and as a force of nature, in films that have fluctuated in their views of the kaiju king, treating Godzilla sometimes with deadly seriousness, then shifting tone to depict the uber-lizard in a far more lightweight, even humorous fashion.

American half sheet poster for Godzilla, King of the Monsters!

With 2024 marking the 70th anniversary of the release of the first Godzilla film, plus a new Japanese film, *Godzilla Minus One*, hitting cinemas and getting rave reviews, not to mention the ongoing success of Big G in a string of smash hit, big budget American movies (and there's the live action US TV series *Monarch: Legacy of Monsters* too), now is just the time to have a look back at this cool, characterful creature, who is an international icon and one of the most famous and recognisable symbols of Japanese popular culture...

Japanese film company Toho was motivated to make the original *Godzilla* movie following the box office successes of *The Beast from 20,000 Fathoms* (1953) and the re-release of 1933's *King Kong* in 1952. *The Beast from 20,000 Fathoms*, with stop-motion special effects by Ray Harryhausen, was the first film to feature a gigantic creature awakened by an atomic bomb explosion, and *Godzilla* (1954) would use a similar concept. The name Godzilla is a romanisation of the Japanese name Gojira, which is a combination of two Japanese words meaning 'gorilla' and 'whale'. The raging, radioactive reptile obviously doesn't resemble a whale or a gorilla, but the name was intended to imply something truly huge, powerful, animalistic and aquatic.

Ishirō Honda directed and co-wrote *Godzilla*, the music was by Akira Ifukube, who composed the famous Godzilla theme, and special effects were supplied by Eiji Tsuburaya, who helped to pioneer the various tokusatsu (special effects) techniques that would be used in subsequent kaiju productions, including the use of scale model buildings and men in monster suits (suitmation).

But what gave *Godzilla* much more gravitas compared to *The Beast from 20,000 Fathoms* was the fact that the Toho movie was produced by a nation that had actually suffered from and lived through two atomic bomb attacks on its cities during World War 2. The titular beast was not just an enormous monster on the loose, he could be viewed as an ominous, living personification of Japan's fears of the threat of radioactivity in this new atomic age.

The look of Godzilla in the first film was that of a bipedal, humongous, dinosaur-like reptile that had jagged Stegosaurus-style plates running along his back and tail. With stout, pillar-like legs, the ability to emit radioactive heat-blasts from his mouth, and a distinctive roar, Godzilla's features have stayed pretty much the same (until *Shin Godzilla*), but with slight (and not so slight) differences from movie to movie, including alterations in Godzilla's facial expressions, a reduction in the amount of toes, the removal and then reincorporation of larger fangs, and overall size fluctuations (Godzilla's size can change from scene to scene in a film sometimes).

The 1954 film was a hit, launching the kaiju eiga (monster movies) genre in Japan. An extensively re-edited version (titled *Godzilla, King of the Monsters!*) was

Nom, nom, nom... train carriages taste good!

Japanese poster for Gojira (Godzilla)

UK quad poster for Godzilla, King of the Monsters!

released in America in 1956. This featured over 20 minutes of new footage, starring Raymond Burr playing journalist Steve Martin, which was edited into the original Japanese movie. (The habit of incorporating a Western actor became fairly routine in subsequent tokusatsu kaiju films, such as with the US releases of *Half Human*, *Gamera the Giant Monster* and *King Kong vs. Godzilla*).

Whatever you think about *Godzilla, King of the Monsters!*, this was the version of the film that was responsible for introducing Godzilla to an international audience. In Great Britain the movie was slapped with an 'X' certificate, for adults only.

The Godzilla franchise would go from strength to strength, with the popularity of the movies leading to Godzilla appearing in other types of media, including cartoons, music, books, magazines, comics, toys, model kits and video games.

The Godzilla film series is broken down into four different 'eras'. The first, second, and fourth eras are named after the Japanese emperor who was reigning during production: the Shōwa era (Emperor Shōwa is known as Emperor Hirohito in English), the Heisei era (the period corresponding to the reign of Emperor Emeritus Akihito), and the Reiwa era (when the then-crown prince Naruhito ascended to the throne). The third era is called the Millennium era, because the Emperor (Heisei) was the same, but these Godzilla movies are considered to have a different style and they feature storylines that differ a lot from the Heisei era flicks.

Shōwa era (1954 - 1975)

The first series of movies started with 1954's *Godzilla* and ended with 1975's *Terror of Mechagodzilla*.

After 1955's sequel *Godzilla Raids Again* (re-edited and released as *Gigantis, the Fire Monster* in the US), which first featured the staple of having Godzilla battling it out with another massive monster (in this case the ankylosaur-like Anguirus), the Godzilla films from then on would be shot in colour, starting with the hugely profitable *King Kong vs. Godzilla* (1962).

The genesis of *King Kong vs. Godzilla* is interesting, in that it was originally a project conceived by stop-motion effects master Willis O'Brien as a sequel to *King Kong* (1933), with the big ape coming face to face with an equally enormous Frankenstein Monster. The film would've been titled *King Kong vs. Prometheus*. O'Brien's story idea was stolen by producer John Beck, who sold it to Toho, who ultimately made *King Kong vs. Godzilla* instead. O'Brien did contemplate suing Beck for intent to defraud, but he did not have enough money for a protracted legal battle. *King Kong vs. Godzilla* was released theatrically in Japan on August 11th, 1962, and O'Brien died of a heart attack in his home on November 10th, 1962. His widow, Darlyne, would later cite "the frustration of the King Kong Vs. Frankenstein deal" as a contributing factor to his death.

In this movie Godzilla was still depicted as the villain, breaking free of an iceberg to cause havoc. The film was colourful and a lot of fun, though King Kong purists will no doubt continue to frown and wince when looking at the rather inexpressive mask used for the heroic ape, which only showed any movement in a handful of close-ups, where a separate head was utilised to show Kong doing such things as eating berries.

With shots of Kong being floated to his showdown with Godzilla by balloons (an updated version of this Kong airlift occurs in 2021's US MonsterVerse flick *Godzilla vs. Kong*), and a fight with a big octopus, the movie's real highpoint is the super-fight on Mount Fuji. This finale has a lot of oomph to it, as Kong gets trashed, knocked to the ground, covered in boulders, and smacked about the cranium by Godzilla's tail. Then... an electrical storm appears, lightning strikes Kong, he absorbs its power, his face glows blue, and he really lays into the radioactive reptile, his every touch giving

off bolts of electricity, whilst trees burn about the beasts thanks to Godzilla's bad breath. Fun, fun, fun!

1964's *Mothra vs. Godzilla* (also known as *Godzilla vs. The Thing*), dealing with issues like corporate greed, nuclear testing, themes of unity and mysticism, is considered to be one of Ishiro Honda's best Godzilla entries. Huge insect-deity Mothra, seen previously in her own movie *Mothra* (1961), battles Godzilla, and then, after her demise, her two newborn larvae take over, entrapping Godzilla in their silk. Godzilla was still clearly a menacing, destructive monster at this point of the series, but things would change with the next release...

Beginning with *Ghidorah, the Three-Headed Monster* (1964), Godzilla started to change into a more positive, anti-hero-type critter. The large, golden-skinned, winged space-dragon King Ghidorah would become one of Godzilla's key enemies, returning again and again to face-off against Godzilla. Producing hurricane-force winds by flapping its wings, the massive, twin-tailed Ghidorah is usually such a handful that Godzilla often teams-up with other monsters to battle his nemesis, as happens here when the new Mothra and titanic pterosaur Rodan both join up to aid Godzilla.

Invasion of Astro-Monster (1965), also known as *Monster Zero*, *Invasion of the Astro-Monsters*, *Invasion of Planet X* and *Battle of the Astros*, saw Ghidorah return, referred to here as Monster Zero, in a film boasting some good UFO miniature work and nice cartoon laser/sound-wave FX. A high point involves a three-way monster fight between Godzilla, Rodan and King Ghidorah on Planet X's rocky surface, with Godzilla doing a preposterous victory dance after seeing off King Ghidorah! With devious, shades-wearing aliens using the monsters to attack Earth, *Invasion of Astro-Monster* ends with King Ghidorah being given a good beating-up by Godzilla and Rodan. Great stuff!

Ebirah, Horror of the Deep (1966), aka *Godzilla vs. the Sea Monster*, was an entertaining yarn (originally planned to star King Kong before the ape was replaced with Godzilla) that featured a villainous group called the Red Bamboo, based on an island guarded by a giant lobster! Not to be taken seriously, the film's best moment for me was the confrontation between Godzilla and his shrimpy adversary, where they take turns smacking a huge boulder at

Godzilla fights Ebirah!

A cool Kamacuras from *Son of Godzilla* (1967)

each other, as if they're playing volleyball! This bright, tightly-budgeted, lightweight production also had a brief fight between Godzilla and a giant condor, a nuclear power plant getting smashed, and a cameo from Mothra.

Son of Godzilla (1967) came next, and it was another colourful, island-set story. This time we got some wonderfully entertaining monsters brought to life as marionettes, rather than men in suits. The Kamacuras were three mutated giant praying mantises, and Kumonga was an eight-legged, massive, web-spitting spider. These puppet beasts are great fun to watch, especially the mantises. The other new creature that appeared in this Godzilla flick, which I definitely found less appealing to watch, was Minilla... Godzilla's son! Obviously intended to appeal to younger audiences, this pug-faced lil' bugger blew smoke rings, made babyish noises and was meant to be cuddly and cute, but I've always found the critter (also referred to in some dubs as Minya) to be rather annoying... and it doesn't even resemble Godzilla! Talking of which, the Godzilla suit used in this entry has a goofy, toad-like face. But, hey, the big bug monsters are the main reasons for watching this playful flick.

All Monsters Attack (1969), also known as *Godzilla's Revenge*, was another release to really aim at the kiddie audience, and is disliked by many for cutting costs and just regurgitating footage from previous Toho films (*Ebirah, Horror of the Deep*, *King Kong Escapes*, *Son of Godzilla*, etc). Focusing on a childish tale of a young boy dreaming that he can visit Monster Island and become pals with Minilla, who can shrink down to human size and chat with him, the film's new monster footage involved a bullying beast called Gabara, a somewhat foolish-looking creature who fights Minilla and Godzilla. With a message about standing up to bullies, *All Monsters Attack*, though much maligned, was a sweet flick that probably doesn't quite deserve all the vitriol it received.

Released the previous year was *Destroy All Monsters* (1968), a very entertaining example of Toho's Shōwa-era kaiju flicks: a universe where monsters are an everyday occurrence, the suits worn by astronauts are bright yellow, cities are regularly wiped-out (but always reconstitute themselves for the next film) and the various armed forces are always on standby with numerous rocket launchers, jets and tanks (which pretty much never have the proper firepower to really hurt the monsters!) In *Destroy All Monsters* we see Godzilla, Rodan, Mothra (larval stage), Anguirus, Gorosaurus, Manda and other kaiju denizens of Monsterland (also known as Monster Island) becoming the pawns of an alien race, called the Kilaaks, who use mind-control devices to turn the (now quite benign) creatures into aggressive, city-wrecking weapons of mass destruction.

With not as much man-in-monster-suit action as you'd think, *Destroy All Monsters* was still a staggeringly fun production, with cell-animated laser effects, some sweet model work, a satisfyingly large quota of monsters, and a knockabout final fight near Mount Fuji, where the re-grouped Earth super-critters kicked and bit Ghidorah the three-headed space dragon until he was well and truly mullered!

By far the best two portions of the film are the opening scenes, where we get a tour of Monsterland that shows us all the great beasties chilling out on their island home, and, of course, the aforementioned no holds barred multi-monster battle

Take a DNA test, Godzilla, this ain't your son!

sequence at the end. Stonkingly amazing entertainment!

1971's *Godzilla vs. Hedorah*, also known as *Godzilla vs. the Smog Monster*, was another shift of tone, telling the story of an ever-changing alien creature that arrived on Earth to devour the world's pollution. It then begins to expel toxic killer mists and sludge-globs! Psychedelic, hippyish, trippy moments, animated interludes, a worthy environmental message backed up by numerous shots of muddy, pollution-ravaged Tokyo bay, a monstrous adversary that sometimes resembles a flying lump of muck with eyes, and scenes of victims getting turned into skeletons, were all mixed together to make this into a quite bizarre, nightmarishly cheesy outing for Godzilla, who even gets to 'fly' in an embarrassing scene that shows the heroic reptile using his atomic breath as a kind of jet propulsion! Oh, the madness of it all!

Godzilla vs. Gigan (aka *War of the Monsters* and *Godzilla on Monster Island*), from 1972, was a far less grim entry and is a real hoot. The film saw Godzilla, with best beast pal Anguirus, take on King Ghidorah and Gigan, who have been sent to attack Japan by alien cockroaches. The space monster Gigan, a bio-mechanical critter with buzzsaw-like gut-spikes, a beak, metal mandibles, a large back-fin, curved prongs for hands, and a kind of glowing visor instead of eyes, is a truly ludicrous-looking design... and I love it!

The best bit comes when Godzilla does the 'Ali Shuffle' as he 'boxes' with King Ghidorah. The silliest thing in *Godzilla vs. Gigan*, however, is the scene where Godzilla and Anguirus have a chat together! Word balloons were used in the Japanese version, but the US release uses actual English-dubbed voices. There was an over-use of stock footage in this film again, that's for sure, but you do get to see Godzilla bleed from wounds and, of course, you also get to see silly ol' Gigan! And, hooray, Gigan returned in the next movie, *Godzilla vs. Megalon* (1973)! This flick, which was guilty of reusing stock footage too, has a story that revolves around the denizens of the undersea kingdom of Seatopia, who are hopping mad about the repeated nuclear tests on Earth that have disturbed their tranquility... so they decide to unleash a monster named Megalon topside to wreck lots of stuff.

Megalon is another unhinged Toho monster design: it has a bug-like face, beetle-wings on its back, and a central

GIANT AGAINST GIANT... the ultimate battle!

GODZILLA vs MEGALON

This doesn't actually happen in the movie, okay?

Page 29 Film Frenzy

Titanosaurus!

Mechagodzilla!

GODZILLA VS. MECHAGODZILLA

Criterion Collection artwork by Takashi Okazaki

projection sticking from the top of its head (inspired by the long cephalic horn of the Japanese rhinoceros beetle), from which it can fire yellow lightning bolts. The mad-lookin' monster also has metallic forearm appendages, which can be combined to form a single rotating drill, allowing the beastie to speedily burrow underground!

The oddball, absurd, bio-mechanical look of Megalon's design certainly put the bug-eyed beast in the same category as the cyborg-kaiju Gigan, which is cool as Gigan arrives to team-up with Megalon in this film, to do battle with Godzilla, who joins forces with Jet Jaguar, a humanoid (Ultraman knock-off) robot that can grow from human size to kaiju dimensions! Big G and Jet Jaguar are ultimately victorious, of course, forcing Megalon and Gigan to retreat, after which Godzilla and Jet Jaguar shake each other's hands and go their separate ways! They're mates! Was this movie silly, ludicrous and cheap? You bet! But it is all kinds of fun too, with a splendidly cheesy, loopy, mad suitmation-tastic third act WWE-style fight, where Godzilla (with a face like a giant, cheeky gecko) performs two jaw-droppingly exaggerated, gravity-defying drop kicks!

The final two Godzilla films to be released as part of the Shōwa era both featured the fan-favourite robo-kaiju... Mechagodzilla!

Godzilla vs. Mechagodzilla (1974), also known as *Godzilla vs. Bionic Monster* and *Godzilla vs. Cosmic Monster*, which came out to celebrate Godzilla's 20th anniversary, presented us with the massive reptilian hero tackling his mechanical doppelgänger, controlled by alien apes! Failing to beat his robo-twin in combat on his own, Godzilla is assisted by dog-faced Okinawan god-monster King Caesar (aka King Seeser). Godzilla's beastly buddy Angiurus returns, and is shown to be capable of leaping at his foes now, leading to a very physical skirmish with Mechagodzilla. Mecha-G is definitely the stand-out element in this film, firing rockets from its fingers, discharging lightning bolts from its chest, emitting colourful beams from its eyes, and creating whirling forcefields with its spinning metal head! The fights are really enjoyable, full of multiple explosions and animated power beams. Even Mechagodzilla's knees are lethal, as they fire projectiles at Godzilla and King Caesar!

Terror of Mechagodzilla (1975), also known as *Monsters from an Unknown Planet*, has Godzilla combating a new

Mechagodzilla (controlled again by the extraterrestrial ape-beings), with the mecha-monster this time helped by a long-necked kaiju-dinosaur called Titanosaurus, an aquatic behemoth capable of creating powerful winds with its webbed tail! Titanosaurus could often look pretty goofy in its scenes, but I still like the beast!

Even though Toho brought back Ishirô Honda to direct and Akira Ifukube to compose the great score, *Terror of Mechagodzilla* performed poorly at the box office, leading to an almost decade-long hiatus in the series.

Heisei era (1984 - 1995)

The series was rebooted with *The Return of Godzilla* in 1984, which ignored every movie after the 1954 original, taking on a darker and more serious tone.

The film's dialogue often deals with musings concerning whether or not the great reptile is somehow a terrible offspring of man's pride and carelessness, here to remind us of just how puny we are. All these deep meditations were a far cry from the 70s-era Godzilla flicks, where a valiant, do-gooder Godzilla fought cockroach aliens and Minilla taught children how to deal with bullies, so, in the context of *The Return of Godzilla*, it made a lot of sense to ignore all the films that came after the original.

Godzilla is still obviously a suitmation creation here, but the sets are more spectacular, and there is a pretty respectable fight with fighter jets. Scenes of the main actors attempting to escape a wrecked skyscraper work well, imbuing the enterprise with a disaster movie feel.

New World Pictures produced an edited English-language version titled *Godzilla 1985*, which added Raymond Burr, reprising his role of Steve Martin from *Godzilla, King of the Monsters!* Burr's scenes look tacked-on, though, and really could've been done without.

Godzilla vs. Biollante (1989) featured a plant monster created by a scientist who spliced cells from his dead daughter and some Godzilla cells into a rose. Bad idea! This genetically altered plant-animal hybrid kaiju appears in different forms, at first resembling a giant rose with long, prehensile vines and a set of jaws inside a large, red flower. Its second

It's all kicking off in *The Return of Godzilla!*

Godzilla fights the huge plant-animal monster Biollante!

Godzilla vs. King Ghidorah (1991)

remove a carnivorous dinosaur (Godzillasaurus) from an island before it could be mutated into Godzilla by the Castle Bravo H-bomb test conducted at the nearby Bikini Atoll in 1954. The future folk turn out to actually have ulterior motives, however, and their real plan results in the creation of King Ghidorah!

The triple-necked, winged menace really looks good in this film! King Ghidorah battles Godzilla, but loses its middle head and its wings get wrecked, leaving the beast in a comatose state.... but its remains are salvaged and the critter is revived as... Mecha-King Ghidorah! This cyborg iteration of the great dragon-monster sports a robot middle head, plus mechanical neck, chest, wings, knees and tail-tips! Mecha-King Ghidorah's cybernetic central head can fire a triple laser beam from the cannon housed in its mouth, the cyborg-beast can also deploy four electrified capture-cables, and even possesses a big mechanical hand with which it can grab onto Godzilla!

The success of *Godzilla vs. King Ghidorah* at the box office inspired Toho to start reintroducing classic monsters from the Shōwa series into these Heisei Godzilla movies. And so it was time for a certain Lepidopterous kaiju to be reintroduced...

Godzilla vs. Mothra (1992), also known as *Godzilla and Mothra: The Battle for Earth*, showcased the return of everybody's favourite divine moth: Mothra! Also appearing in this film, for Godzilla to battle, was a more destructive dark deity moth-monster called Battra! This critter had yellow horns on its head and wings that were more ragged and evil-looking. As this film involved Mothra, we got some preachy save-the-environment messages, a chance to see the new micro-sized twin priestesses of Mothra (called the 'Cosmos'), and scenes of both Mothra and Battra in their larval forms. Lots of fighting and colourful special effects abound in this film (and the popular Mothra would go on to star in her own trilogy of 90s movies).

Godzilla vs. Mechagodzilla II (1993) saw Toho bring back their good ol' robo-zilla character, though I have to admit I preferred the meaner-faced look of the 70s version of Mechagodzilla. The reason the filmmakers made Mechagodzilla (who has been reverse-engineered from the remains of Mecha-King Ghidorah in this story) look less evil now is probably down to the fact that this cyber-critter is actually a good guy in the movie. Godzilla gets to skirmish with famed pterosaur-kaiju Rodan in this flick too, plus there is also the return of... BabyGodzilla! No!!! Ah, but wait, this BabyGodzilla monster suit is infinitely better-looking than the pug-faced costume used for the mewling, annoying Minilla back in the 70s. In the following two films BabyGodzilla would grow up to be first LittleGodzilla and then a sub-adult, named Godzilla Junior, but I digress, let's get back to *Godzilla vs. Mechagodzilla II*... This entry features the international joint military organization known as G-Force, there's lots of chaos and destruction, the seemingly

form develops more reptilian attributes: a long-snouted, tooth-filled, crocodilian head, lots of tendrils and vines, some of which have dangerously-sharp ends and others that terminate in small, toothy mouths! This massive kaiju only appeared in this one live action Godzilla movie, but it remains a fan favourite.

1991's *Godzilla vs. King Ghidorah* saw the return of Big G's three-headed nemesis! The story involves time travellers from the future arriving in Japan to say that they are going to save the country from Godzilla by heading back to 1944 to

Mecha-King Ghidorah strikes!

dead Rodan is resurrected as the red-skinned Fire Rodan, and we get to witness the damaged Mechagodzilla being modified to become Super MechaGodzilla!

G-Force would build yet another anti-Godzilla machine in 1994's *Godzilla vs. SpaceGodzilla*, this time calling it MOGUERA (an acronym for Mobile Operations Godzilla Universal Expert Robot Aero-type). This drill-nosed robotic machine, which was actually a reimagining of the robo-monster seen in Toho's 1957 sci-fi flick *The Mysterians*, actually ends up fighting with Godzilla, rather than against him, to combat the bigger threat posed by SpaceGodzilla.

SpaceGodzilla is an interesting creation, closely resembling Godzilla (it was spawned when some of Big G's cells ended up in space), but with massive, glowing crystals thrusting from its back. This extraterrestrial beastie, with its energy attacks, psychic powers, and its ability to create and use crystals in varying ways, was a very resilient, tough opponent for Godzilla.

This entertaining film marked Godzilla's 40th anniversary and also featured LittleGodzilla (blech!), Fairy Mothra and Mothra (plus stock footage of Battra and Biollante).

The final Heisei era Godzilla movie was *Godzilla vs. Destoroyah* (1995), which I like a lot. Directed by Takao Okawara, with a script written by Kazuki Omori and special effects by Koichi Kawakita, this film saw Godzilla, coated in hot, glowing, lava-like rashes, going on a wrecking spree in Hong Kong. It is revealed that Godzilla's internal nuclear fission processes have gone haywire, threatening to explode and destroy the world. If this wasn't bad enough, another monster has appeared: a creature that is a conglomeration of masses of crustaceans that were mutated by the Oxygen Destroyer weapon used to kill the very first Godzilla back in 1954.

Destoroyah is a novel, nasty kaiju, becoming a massive beast with a large, central head-horn, glowing orange eyes, big tusks projecting from its face, huge shoulder horns and massive wings. Godzilla bests this beast, which had killed Big G's son, Godzilla Junior, but Destoroyah returns to fight, as a swarm of multiple-legged mini-Destoroyahs! Even after Godzilla wipes out these things, Destoroyah returns yet again in winged form. But Destoroyah is eventually killed and the terminally overheating Godzilla stands alone, dying... so the Japanese Self Defence Force desperately shoot cryo-lasers and fire coolant-projectiles to prevent a full-on meltdown. As an Akira Ifukube theme, reworked with choral voices, plays on the soundtrack, Godzilla roars while his flesh falls off him and he decays... and the human characters watch on as radiation levels rapidly reduce... and the camera moves through the smoke and steam and there, backlit, is Godzilla Junior, who has been brought back to life by his dying father's energies, and has rapidly matured, ready to take on the role of king of the monsters. This is truly the most emotional moment in Godzilla history! I'm welling-up as I write about it!

This was an awesome way to end the Heisei-era Godzilla series, with a very memorable-looking Godzilla, who was in pain much of the time, glowing with uncontrollable inner-heat, emitting steam, bleeding lava, his great back-plates uncontrollably flickering.

Millennium era (1999 - 2004)

Toho put the Godzilla series on a temporary pause, to make space for TriStar Pictures' big budget US *Godzilla* movie, which was eventually released in 1998. The widespread fan backlash against Dean Devlin and Roland Emmerich's take on the property, plus newfound demand for a Japanese-made Godzilla film, persuaded Toho to release a new live action entry in the series, titled *Godzilla 2000: Millennium*, in 1999, which started the third era of Godzilla films, known as the Millennium series. The Millennium era Godzilla films can be viewed as an anthology series, because most of these films were standalone stories, with the 1954 film acting as the only previous point of reference. Just *Godzilla Against Mechagodzilla* and *Godzilla: Tokyo S.O.S.* share continuity with each other.

In *Godzilla 2000: Millennium*, aka *Godzilla 2000*, we got to see the new-look Godzilla suit, which boasted large, sharp back-plates, a head with a toothy, big mouth, a somewhat flattened cranium, and eyes positioned further towards the front of the very reptilian-looking face.

Here Godzilla is like a living force of nature, forever being tracked by a Japanese organisation called the Godzilla

Stunning artwork for the US *Godzilla 2000* poster

Godzilla, Mothra and King Ghidorah!

Prediction Network. Meanwhile, an ancient UFO, discovered within a big rock, is eventually revealed to have occupants who crave the regenerative substance contained in Godzilla's cells. The UFO finally absorbs Godzilla's DNA, which is transferred to its occupants, who transform into a single tentacled life form that exits the UFO. The octo-alien, rendered via some just-about-acceptable CGI effects, starts to mutate due to the volatile effects of Godzilla's DNA, and it transforms into an enormous kaiju with gigantic, clawed hands. This beast, known as Orga, looks pretty damn good, because it is a practical suitmation creation augmented with digital effects. Orga continues to mutate, finally developing dorsal-plates and an extendable maw that starts to swallow Godzilla whole, but Godzilla releases pent-up energy and destroys the massive monster!

A memorable moment early in this movie has characters rapidly reversing their vehicle along a road tunnel, with Godzilla's huge foot repeatedly smashing through the tunnel ceiling as Big G pursues them. The film, all in all, was a solid start to the new series.

Meanwhile, in the story continuity of Godzilla vs. Megaguirus (2000), Japan has been attacked repeatedly by Godzilla since 1954. The new Japanese capital is in Osaka, where the government forms a special unit that creates a weapon called the Dimension Tide, a miniature black hole gun designed to trap Godzilla within another dimension. The weapon is test-fired, a wormhole is created, which allows a Meganula (a big, prehistoric dragonfly) to reach present day Tokyo via a time distortion, where it lays an egg, from which swarms of Meganulon (monster dragonfly nymphs) hatch and begin to attack people in the city. These insectoid beasts moult their skins and transform into Meganula dragonflies, which steal energy from Godzilla and transfer it to their queen, transforming her into the gigantic Megaguirus. I hope you followed all that!

Suffice to say, Godzilla must fight the fast-flying, stinger-wielding Megaguirus and contend with the human forces who are eager to blast him with their black hole weapon.

2001's Godzilla, Mothra and King Ghidorah: Giant Monsters All-Out Attack (now there's a mouthful), also known as Godzilla, Mothra and King Ghidorah: Attack of the Giant Monsters (now there's another mouthful), gave us yet another continuity reboot to the series. This movie was directed by Shusuke Kaneko, the man behind the wonderful, acclaimed Gamera (Heisei) Trilogy of movies (yes, Kaneko made Daiei Film's giant flying turtle hero into a really cool kaiju!)

In this entry, Godzilla faces-off against three guardian monsters: Baragon (the burrowing, horned kaiju last seen in Destroy All Monsters), Mothra, and King Ghidorah. The creature fights are pretty violent here, and the special effects are good. The film received a lot of praise, although some fans weren't happy that King Ghidorah was a good kaiju in this story and Godzilla was portrayed as the full-on badass villain. Nevertheless, Godzilla, Mothra and King Ghidorah: Giant Monsters All-Out Attack ended up being the most successful Godzilla film of the Millennium era.

Godzilla Against Mechagodzilla (2002) was, you guessed it, yet another reboot to the Godzilla continuity. The movie reintroduced everyone's favourite robo-zilla into the Millennium series, but this time the cyborg was created using the skeleton and DNA of the first, dead Godzilla (from 1954). Codenamed Kiryu, this bio-mechanical beast turned on its human controllers when Godzilla's roar awakened the first Godzilla's soul residing within the mecha-monster, enabling it to possess the machine!

Kiryu is repaired, eventually being guided by human pilot First Lieutenant Akane Yashiro in a battle with Godzilla, using a powerful Absolute Zero Cannon to fight

Godzilla: Final Wars (2004)

Godzilla: Final Wars (2004)

Godzilla: Final Wars (2004)

Godzilla to a draw... meaning that the next film, Godzilla: Tokyo S.O.S. (2003), is a direct sequel and not another story reboot!

This follow-up flick involves fights between Godzilla, Kiryu, Mothra and two of her larvae. The itsy-bitsy Shobijin (the priestesses of Mothra) show up to say that the first Godzilla's bones (used to build the cyborg-beast Kiryu, remember?) must be returned to the sea, because kaiju-deity Mothra considers the use of these bones in a machine to be sacrilegious and against the natural order of things. After various battles and the death of momma Mothra, Yashiro flies an injured Godzilla across the ocean and plunges the cyborg-zilla beneath the waves, thus returning the original Godzilla's bones to their watery grave. Godzilla: Tokyo S.O.S. features another monster, albeit just a carcass washed up on a beach: a Kamoebas giant turtle, which is the same species of creature also seen in Toho's kaiju film Space Amoeba (1970).

The sixth and final instalment in the Millennium series was Godzilla: Final Wars (2004). Directed by Ryuhei Kitamura, the man behind such entertaining, stylised genre flicks as Versus, Azumi and Sky High, the film commemorates the 50th anniversary of the Godzilla franchise by featuring LOADS of kaiju! It is a fast-paced production that reaches levels of near-lunacy that some Godzilla purists may frown upon, but I love this immensely enjoyable monster mash!

Here's just some of the outlandish stuff that happens in this film...

Godzilla is confronted with Zilla, the iteration of Godzilla seen in Roland Emmerich's much-derided 1998 US Godzilla movie, has a super-brief skirmish with this CGI critter, then hurls Zilla into an exploding Sydney Opera House: boom! Gigan, looking trimmer, sharper and cooler, faces-off against Godzilla with new cable-firing abilities, but he soon loses his head! The flying, drill-nosed warship Gotengo (first seen in 1963's Atragon) is commanded by Captain Douglas Gordon (Don Frye), who is the spitting image of Joseph Stalin! In New Guinea, Godzilla swings spider-kaiju Kumonga around and around on its own web, then hurls it over the horizon! Monster X, the most powerful kaiju controlled by the evil Xilien aliens, mutates into Keizer Ghidorah, which gives Big G a sound beating with the gravity beams it spews from its mouths, but Godzilla soon mauls, decapitates and blows-up the beast! And, best of all, Godzilla battles Rodan, Anguirus and dog-eared King Caesar, resulting in hilariously over-the-top hijinks as Anguirus rolls-up into a spiky ball and propels himself at Godzilla, who whacks him away with his tail, and King Caesar retaliates by kicking the spike-ball like a pro-footballer, booting curled-up Anguirus straight at Godzilla, who attempts to grab hold of him like a goalkeeper!

Other kaiju featured in the flick include Manda, Hedorah, Minilla (gawd) and Kamacuras.

Ryuhei Kitamura manages to make Godzilla: Final Wars slick, cheesy, fun, exciting and silly, all at once. Some of his characters have the same kind of glam, hip vibe as the protagonists and antagonists seen in his other movies, such as Versus, and he somehow succeeds in being both respectful and disrespectful to the Godzilla franchise: the movie is an absolutely ridiculous, outlandish, don't-give-a-f*ck joy!

Reiwa era (2016 - present)

Toho put the Godzilla series on hold after the release of Godzilla: Final Wars, though director Yoshimitsu (Godzilla vs. Hedorah) Banno attempted to raise money to make a short IMAX Godzilla film called Godzilla 3-D. This project never came to fruition, but Banno's attempts to secure funding, together with producers Kenji Okuhira and Brian Rogers, led to US company Legendary Entertainment acquiring the rights to the Godzilla character in 2010, resulting in the creation of the American MonsterVerse movie series, beginning with Godzilla (2014). The American film was an international success, and Toho finally decided to make a new Godzilla movie of their own, called Shin Godzilla (2016), which was the first Japanese Godzilla movie of the Reiwa era.

Shin Godzilla was a huge critical and financial smash in Japan. Some western fans, however, bemoaned the amount of time the film spent with the politicians and bureaucrats, but I think that watching how all the many viewpoints, red tape and opinions swamped the decision makers contributed lots of realism to the story.

The movie adds new twists to Godzilla's lifecycle, with the creature evolving through different forms, which I personally liked: you can't just keep doing the same old schtick every time. In this iteration of the Big G

Shin Godzilla (2016) — I find this shot quite disturbing for some reason!

Shin Godzilla (2016) — Such weird, lidless, unblinking eyes...

Shin Godzilla (2016) — Shin Godzilla ain't pretty!

the city seen in extreme long shot, giving us an expansive view of the creature's progress through Tokyo.

And I loved the way the Japanese forces not only use tanks, helicopters and jets against Godzilla... they also utilised 'train bombs' - cool!

There were some odd design choices, I agree, like the early-stage googly fish eyes, for instance, but, as already stated, I think there was a lot to enjoy with this version of Godzilla, who, once in adult form, looks quite different to his typical body shape, with very tiny eyes and a longer neck. Shin Godzilla was the first Japanese Godzilla to be rendered primarily through CGI, though he somehow retains a slight suitmation vibe, maybe because actor Mansai Nomura portrayed Godzilla through motion capture.

As the Reiwa era continued we got a trilogy of anime Godzilla movies, with Netflix distributing the films worldwide. The cartoon films, which had cinema releases in Japan, were *Godzilla: Planet of the Monsters* (2017), *Godzilla: City on the Edge of Battle* (2018) and *Godzilla: The Planet Eater* (2018).

For me, the plotting in these films is needlessly convoluted. For instance, in the first story, the monsters menace Earth just as aliens turn up and then everyone leaves, then come back thousands of years later. It doesn't help that Godzilla moves around that slowly he sucks all the vitality from many of the scenes in this trilogy. Having said all that, *Godzilla: The Planet Eater*, despite suffering from far, far too much chat in the earlier part of the movie, does become extremely interesting once King Ghidorah arrives. This version of Ghidorah is from another dimension and it functions in ways that confound the laws of our dimension's physics. Only seen as three glowing heads on very long necks that sinuously extrude from singularities hovering amongst the clouds, Ghidorah is only able to manifest itself here because

we see him transform from a low-sprawling aquatic beast to upright god-reptile. We watch him continually adapt, utilising atomic breath and then photon beams. Maybe old school Godzilla fans might not like this updating of his abilities, but I thought the ever-evolving powers and adaptations kept the story intriguing (such as that last shot of the tail hinting that an even weirder evolutionary step was underway within the great beast).

The devastation shots of boats & debris being pushed down the river effectively replicated real disaster imagery seen during the 2011 Japanese tsunami, and I liked the many scenes of Godzilla stomping through

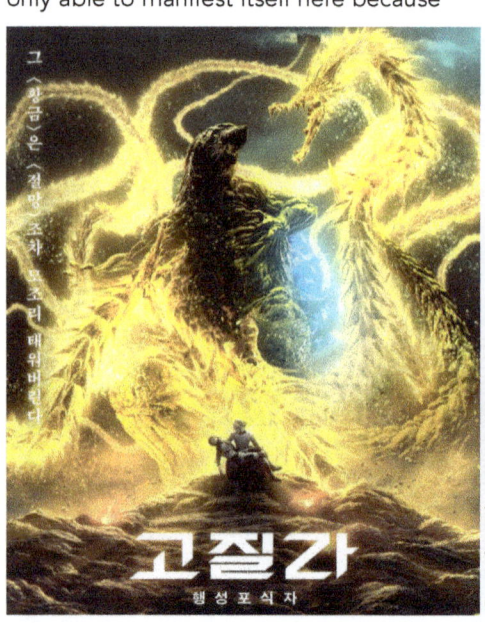

ACTORS WITHIN THE BEAST

Here are some of the hard-working guys who have donned the heavy, iconic costumes to play Godzilla...

Haruo Nakajima - An actor and stuntman who played Godzilla in the first 12 films, from 1954 to 1972.

Tsutomu Kitagawa - Wore the huge, scaly suit for five of the Millennium series of Godzilla films.

Kenpachiro Satsuma - Played Godzilla in *The Return of Godzilla* (1984) and in all of the Heisei films.

Satsuma passed away recently, on December 16th, 2023. RIP

Mizuho Yoshida - Was Big G in *Godzilla, Mothra and King Ghidorah: Giant Monsters All-Out Attack* (2001).

---

the triple-headed world-destroyer is being observed by a specific character, which is an explanation that leans quite heavily into quantum physics concepts. The finale becomes a tour de force of metaphysical mutterings, flashbacks, and great shots of Ghidorah's other-dimensional heads as they entangle and bite Godzilla, siphoning away all of his energies!

These three anime films all certainly look good and involve some cool future-tech contraptions, but I'm much more interested in Toho's latest live action film, *Godzilla Minus One*. This film, which is set in a wrecked, devastated postwar Japan, ramps up the melodramatic aspects of the story, and shows the events from the point of view of the everyday people. I was very impressed with this movie, which made me really care a lot about the protagonists, and it also features the most devastating depiction of Godzilla's radioactive breath!

The eras...

There are films that I like from all four eras, but I guess I have a real soft spot for the Shōwa era, no doubt because it spans a lot more films, with big shifts in tone and themes. From the dark, serious, symbolism-heavy, doom-laden *Godzilla* (1954), to the colourful, more juvenile releases like *Godzilla vs. Gigan* and *All Monsters Attack*, there's such a mind-bogglingly vast difference in style between them that it adds to the overall enjoyment of this era's releases. Godzilla himself morphs from an unstoppable force of nature, to anti-hero, to caring parent!

Godzilla movies can be enjoyed for all sorts of reasons. The stories can sometimes have political themes, whilst others go to town with backstories featuring quite in-depth internal mythologies, and others, of course, are simply no-nonsense action-sci-fi movies that include everything from ape-aliens, space-cockroaches, hi-tech military gizmos and a menagerie of massive monsters. Maybe the human characters in these films are often bland or forgettable, and there will be some viewers who'll never take seriously the way the Toho creatures are brought to life via suitmation techniques. Some Godzilla suits have been far more complex, well-designed and better made than others, that's for sure, but, hey, I like 'em all!

Even at the most basic man-in-rubber-suit-stomping-on-model-houses level, there's lots to enjoy: it's a sort of cinematic

Godzilla Minus One (2023)

Criterion Collection artwork by Arthur Adams

representation of the kind of enjoyably juvenile joy that one used to have, as a child, when, after building your Lego houses... you wrecked them! This toy-trashing bliss is enhanced by the fact the planes and tanks in some of these flicks actually do look very much like toys, adding to the fun of seeing them get smashed by often absurd-looking creatures: wouldn't you just love to run around a scale model city and do the same thing?!

Godzilla Minus One is obviously far removed from this lo-fi aspect of the Godzilla franchise. It still boasts scenes of cathartic, large-scale property damage and ship-wrecking, though, which is definitely capable of pleasing your inner destructive child!

The American Godzilla movies...

There can be a distinct divide between fans of the Toho Godzilla movies and lovers of the US MonsterVerse flicks. One group of adherents tend to reflexively dismiss the films liked by the others. But what's the point of that? Isn't it wonderful to be a Godzilla movie enthusiast today, with all this Godzilla content to choose from?!

Anyway, here are my thoughts regarding the American Godzilla films...

Godzilla (1998) failed due to the arrogance of Roland Emmerich and Dean Devlin, who came on board the TriStar Godzilla project (which had initially been developed by writers Ted Elliott and Terry Rossio, with Jan De Bont attached to direct) and said that they were only willing to take on the film if they were allowed to totally reinvent Godzilla into something wholly their own. So they ditched the way Elliott and Rossio portrayed Godzilla as a guardian of world ecosystems in a story that would see Godzilla do battle with an evil monster called the Gryphon. Instead, Devlin and Emmerich turned Godzilla into a plain and simple giant creature, like a T-Rex with a jutting chin! They also got rid of all of the other monsters in the screenplay. The finished film did have some decent model effects on show and some of the creature stuff was okay, but so many bad choices were made: Godzilla doesn't look like Godzilla, Godzilla is not big enough, Godzilla RUNS AWAY from the military, Godzilla doesn't have radioactive breath, Godzilla just wants to munch on piles of fish, and Godzilla seems to be just a mutated (French) iguana. Plus, the military are such idiots in this film: they blow up the Flatiron building, they shoot the top off the Chrysler Building with missiles and they torpedo their own subs. If the film had been called something else, and wasn't linked to Godzilla, it would've been better received.

The Gareth Edwards-directed *Godzilla* (2014), the first of Legendary Entertainment's MonsterVerse movies, is much, much better than the '98 version. It can be seen as a movie of many good images & moments, rather than a perfect whole, but the scenes and imagery are really good, such as the view of the inside of a 'cave' that is actually a fossil Godzilla, the heartbreaking scene where Juliette Binoche is locked inside the radioactive steam-filled corridor, the halo dive, the first time we see Godzilla's blue flame breath, and so on. Awesome stuff!

There are some really nice touches, as when Godzilla inadvertently causes a tsunami when he comes ashore because he's so damn big. The finale, when Godzilla is revealed to be alive after killing the MUTOs and everyone cheers the big critter like he's a heroic king of monsters, is also brilliant!

The makers of *Godzilla: King of the Monsters* (2019) certainly set out to create their version of a Japanese kaiju movie writ large: we get gigantic monsters kicking each other's butts, jet attacks, cities flattened, fire and fury.

There are lots of cool elements in this film: using the original Godzilla theme tune (and Mothra's theme plays during the end credits), introducing the Oxygen Destroyer weapon, referencing the Infant Island twins, and much more.

The movie is full of striking images: Ghidorah powering up with electricity zapping out from its wingtips! Godzilla going into action with the backup of military jets! Ghidorah raising its wings atop a mountain like a giant demon (with a crucifix in the foreground)! The remaining monsters bowing in deference to the victorious Godzilla! Yes, there was definitely lots of stuff to like! *Godzilla: King of the Monsters* certainly delivered in the monster department: seeing Godzilla, Mothra, Ghidorah and Rodan in action in a big Hollywood picture was a great experience, plus we got to see several other monsters too, including Behemoth, a bizarre tusked Titan!

Godzilla vs. Kong (2021), directed by Adam Wingard, was certainly a big punch 'em up production, crammed with a neon-lit deluge of eye candy monster effects, including the introduction of the US Mechagodzilla! It delivered on the promise of its title, with the titular creatures duking it out with themselves and others. From a plot perspective it certainly didn't attempt to inject the serious tone of 2014's *Godzilla* and was much more aligned with *Godzilla: King of the Monsters*, where the focus was on creating set-ups to allow for a series a kaiju battles. That said, the 2019 film still attempted to balance the human drama with the scenes of spectacle more evenly than *Godzilla vs. Kong*, which definitely put the emphasis on the grand FX moments. The fantastical elements, like the trip to the Hollow Earth and Kong utilising a powered-up giant axe, were dealt with pretty briskly in this film, and perhaps this was the best way to handle such things – so viewers weren't given too much time to ponder the logic of it all!

The final smackdown battle, taking place in Hong Kong, allowed for gorgeous looking neon vistas that made the night time action easy to follow and see. I have to say I do wonder what the bodycount must have been for this fight as a LOT of skyscrapers get demolished! Maybe aware of this, the film doesn't feature any characters commenting on casualties.

Ultimately, if you go into this just for the spectacle there's lots to like, but there are quite a few things you can pick apart with *Godzilla vs. Kong*. It would've been preferable if the film had developed a more pleasing mix of pulp action, interesting characterisations and monster madness, as seen in the non-Godzilla MonsterVerse release *Kong: Skull Island* (2017).

Godzilla heaven!

For fans of the king of monsters there's never been a better time than now, with both Japanese and American Godzilla movies regularly stomping our way.

Toho's *Godzilla Minus One* thundered into theatres to great acclaim, and now we will have Legendary Entertainment's *Godzilla x Kong: The New Empire* to look forward to when it roars our way soon!

Oh, what wonderful monster-tastic times we now live in!

FILM FRENZY REVIEWS

ASIAN HORROR, FANTASY, SCIENCE FICTION AND CULT MOVIES

THE WITCH: PART 1 - THE SUBVERSION (2018)

Starring Kim Da-mi, Choi Woo-sik, Park Hee-soon, Jo Min-soo, Go Min-si
Written by Park Hoon-jung
Directed by Park Hoon-jung
Goldmoon Film/Peppermint & Company

A young girl escapes from a blood-spattered secret institute, is discovered by a retired couple living on a farm, and is brought up by them as their own child. Ten years later, Koo Ja-yoon (Da-mi), now 19, is encouraged by her friend to audition for a television talent contest, which Ja-yoon agrees to do in the hope of earning money to help her cash-strapped parents. She does very well on the show... but her public appearances attract the attentions of numerous figures linked to the lab that Ja-yoon ran away from.

Written and directed by Park Hoon-jung, this South Korean film initially takes its time, sharing Ja-yoon's ordinary life with us, as she hangs out with her school buddy Myung-hee, sympathetically deals with her mom's dementia symptoms, helps get cattle feed for her father's cows, and suffers from the occasional migraine. All the different characters are efficiently sketched, including Myung-hee's dad, who is the local cop, which helps to draw the viewer into the story, ensuring that we'll care about these folks once the shit hits the fan.

At first Ja-yoon's encounters with the various shady characters, including an initially charming genetically-engineered dude with youthful K-pop star looks (Woo-sik), are only mildly threatening, but the well-handled scenes become more and more menacing, and the tension is expertly ratcheted up until Ja-yoon finally reveals some of her deadly skills when killers from one of the organisation's warring factions pay her a home visit.

Ja-yoon is eventually brought before the gloating Dr Baek (Min-soo), a key figure at the institute that's been creating super-powered operatives, sometimes referred to as 'witches'. These gifted beings have been bred to have heightened physicality and violent natures. Dr Baek tells Ja-yoon that she'd lost her memory ten years ago when she'd escaped from the lab, which is why Ja-yoon took part in the talent show because she was unaware that people were searching for her. Dr Baek points out that Ja-yoon is very lucky. She should be dead: her powers would normally have overloaded her brain by now, causing it to explode, that's why Ja-yoon has migraines, gets nosebleeds, and is becoming more and more ill. Dr Baek injects Ja-yoon with a serum, which she reveals will cure her of her illnesses for one month. She says that she'll keep giving Ja-yoon the serum if she willingly starts to work for the organisation...

...and this is when the movie really impressed me! Suddenly, Ja-yoon's whole demeanour shifts and (spoilers ahead) Dr Baek belatedly grasps that she's been played by this schoolgirl! Ja-yoon, it transpires, has only pretended to have lost her memory for the last ten years! She'd been purposefully underutilising her powers to prevent her brain from overloading and blowing up. Eventually, though, Ja-yoon realised that she would now need this special serum or she would die, so she got herself onto television, then engineered it so that she'd be ID'd, captured and then forcefully made to take the serum... which is what she wanted! The serum re-awakens her brain's full potential and, with a quite disconcerting grin, Ja-yoon goes on the offensive for the rest of the running time!

Okay, so the film had been moving along just fine as it was and I was invested in the story, but this twist, revealing Ja-yoon's long-term planning (which even included 'allowing' the old couple to find & adopt her), made me like *The Witch: Part 1* that much more!

Ja-yoon heads off to seek the formula and a big batch of the serum vials, which will keep her well. This inevitably leads to Ja-yoon clashing with assorted powered operatives in a 3rd act extended showdown set in the abandoned lab she fled from at the start of the film. These slick, savage skirmishes are brutal, thrilling, bloody and well-staged, with the genetically-enhanced characters taking no prisoners as they battle Ja-yoon and fight amongst themselves, tearing into each other in a way you'd never see in a MCU film!

The movie ends with you wanting more, which is fine, as a sequel was made in 2022.

BLOODY MUSCLE BODY BUILDER IN HELL (1995)

Starring Shinichi Fukazawa, Masaaki Kai, Asako Nosaka
Written by Shinichi Fukazawa
Directed by Shinichi Fukazawa
Produced by Shinichi Fukazawa

Naoto (Fukazawa) is asked by his ex-girlfriend, Mika (Nosaka), to take her to the haunted house that Naoto has inherited from his deceased dad. They are accompanied by a psychic (Kai), who is able to pick up on an ominous presence in the building. Later, the face of Naoto's dead father (also played by Fukazawa) appears on a TV screen to warn his son that the psychic is possessed by the ghost of his murdered lover, who has the power to prevent them from leaving the house... and Naoto is informed that the only way to deal with the psychic is to hack him to bits!

This very low budget film from Japan, also known as *The Japanese Evil Dead*, looks really grainy (it was shot on Super 8) and manages to make Sam Raimi's 1981 movie look like a big budget IMAX production in comparison! Shinichi Fukazawa filmed most of this flick in 1995, but it wasn't released on DVD in Japan until 2012. It received an official international release in the UK by Terracotta Distribution in 2017, and since then Visual Vengeance has released the film on Blu-ray in America.

There are lots of lo-fi FX to keep you watching *Bloody Muscle Body Builder In Hell*, such as when the ghost drops a pendant into the psychic's mouth, after which the pendant slithers from the victim's mouth via jerky stop-motion effects, then bores through his eye, into his head! We also get to see a knife rammed through a head, skewering an eyeball on the blade's tip. Some of the visual gore gags are fun, like when Naoto uses his chest expander as a kind of catapult to fire an iron bar through a zombie's head. These effects are far from realistic, but I guess it's the willingness of Fukazawa to try and put this stuff onscreen no matter what that counts.

As much as Fukazawa tries to emulate Sam Raimi's first two *Evil Dead* movies (at one point the lead character even says "Groovy"), there's a lack of real verve and bravura camera techniques compared to Raimi's productions. The location lacks atmosphere too, with everything shot in close-up. But perhaps it's churlish to be too critical about the film's shortcomings, as there's an I'm-doing-the-best-I-can determination to the proceedings, with Fukazawa trying to get as much up on screen as his budget (and his skills) will allow. Thus we get a severed head zipping about on a severed hand, more cheap and cheerful stop-motion footage, and a sequence where the dead girl uses body parts and blood to regrow herself à la a bargain basement version of what happens in *Hellraiser* (1987).

The film ends with shots of a decomposing zombie body, again accomplished by stop-motion and amateur gore effects, that apes the finale of *The Evil Dead* (1981), though it's all done in a far less accomplished way, of course.

If you're partial to do-it-yourself horror productions and you're happy to ignore the many shortcomings, the non-existent budget and a lack of professional technique, then this short, inexpertly-made, unpretentious homage to Sam Raimi's classics just might be your cup of (tarnished) tea.

WARS IN CHINATOWN (2020)

Starring Wang Hongxiang, Wang Zhao, Yue Dongfeng, Shi Xuanru
Written by Guo Yulong
Directed by Guo Yulong
iQIYI Pictures

In early 20th century Shanghai the heroic Ye Zhuo, toting a brutally angular blade, proceeds to decimate droves of fedora-wearing Heilong Gang fighters, all of whom are armed with samurai swords, so that he can reach their boss, Wu Silong, who is holding Ye Zhou's wife captive. In the ensuing face-off between Ye Zhou and Wu Silong, Ye's wife jumps in front of the bullet meant for her husband, prompting a vengeful Ye Zhou to drive his broken blade through Wu Silong's chest. But Ye Zhou finds out that bad guy Wu Silong has somehow survived this killer strike, with the aid of Japanese doctors, and is now residing somewhere in New York... so Ye heads for America too.

Once the story switches to the USA, we're introduced to Chinese newcomer Fang Liang (Zhao) as he moves into a building complex in New York's Chinatown, owned by the gruff Uncle Huang. Fang hangs out with Uncle Huang's daughter Ling and becomes caught up in a dastardly plot involving a Japanese gang conducting experiments on Chinese captives. Ye Zhou soon teams-up with Uncle Huang, Fang Liang and others, including Mr Duan, who makes his own dynamite, and the whole group clashes with the Japanese, who're led by the katana-wielding villainess Tian Hai (Xuanru). This Japanese gang has been working on The Mobile Warrior Plan, a project they hope will help empower Japan in the East, by using super-strong warriors to spearhead Japan's expansion... and the first Mobile Warrior to be successfully created is Wu Silong!

Also known as *Chinatown Wars*, this Chinese film opens with the impactful, bloody Shanghai showdown, and becomes an enjoyably pulpy yarn once the story moves to America, where we are presented with the mystery surrounding Chinese corpses washing up along the river with their hearts removed. We're then introduced to the Japanese baddies in their high-walled HQ, as they test the powers of the bald-headed, emotionless, veiny-faced Mobile Warrior, allowing him to kill a bunch of Chinese captives. Wu Silong later gets an upgrade thanks to a top Japanese scientist pumping the Mobile Warrior full of a special fluid, giving him an undercoating of titanium alloy beneath his skin, making him bulletproof!

These events are all quite diverting and fun to watch: there's a scene with a protagonist called Feng, who is somehow capable of flexing his own backbone until it snaps, thus killing himself so that he doesn't become an experimental test subject!

The less than successful attempt to pass off mainland Chinese sets as locations in New York's Chinatown does let the film down. Later in the story the filmmakers seem to totally forget this movie is meant to be based in New York City as they show the protagonists walking through a goddamn forest to reach Tian Hai's base of operations! A leather-clad Japanese she-fighter, Xun Zi, wears modern-looking gear that doesn't help with the period detail either, but perhaps I'm being too critical of a movie that, let's face it, is hardly attempting to be a realistic drama, focusing as it does on a central plot that involves the creation of indestructible super-dudes!

Yue Dongfeng does a solid job playing the outwardly brusque but valiant Uncle Huang, and I guess Wang Hongxiang ain't bad as the avenging do-gooder Ye Zhou.

The script starts to run out of stream, unfortunately, using a few unsurprising plot beats, involving counterattacks and reprisals, to fill the running time. When the film's finale finally arrives, it concludes with Wu Silong getting fried with electricity until his skin blisters all over. Ye Zhou then stabs his broken blade straight into Wu Silong's chest, just like he did during the Shanghai confrontation at the start of the film, but this time Wu Silong's black heart is knocked out of him and plops onto the floor! This is just the kind of fate we want for the main baddies, so it's a shame that foxy arch nemesis Tian Hai is only shown being offed in a flashback at the end of the film, which reduces any chance of her demise possessing any real impact.

Wars in Chinatown is peppered with a generous helping of martial arts scuffles, gunplay, effectively-staged explosions that hurl stuntmen about the place, and sword-slashing encounters, all of which are done to a decent enough standard, though they ultimately lack the kind of real panache that a better director perhaps could've brought to the proceedings.

THE WITCH: PART 2 - THE OTHER ONE (2022)

Starring Cynthia (Shin Si-ah), Jo Min-soo, Kim Da-mi, Park Eun-bin, Jin Goo
Written by Park Hoon-jung
Directed by Park Hoon-jung
Contents Panda/Next Entertainment World

A genetically enhanced girl (Cynthia) is left for dead in a secret lab where everyone has been wiped out by gas mask-wearing troops. The almost catatonic girl wanders outside and is picked up by gangster Yong-du (Goo) and his men. In the van with the gang is Kyung-hee (Eun-bin), a woman who is refusing to sign away ownership of her house and land to her relative, Yong-du. The girl causes the van to crash and Kyung-hee ends up taking the kid to her house, where Kyung-hee lives with her problematic brother, Dae-gil. From then on the paths of these characters, plus various shady operatives, gangsters and transhuman agents all intersect in a series of ferocious, powered-up encounters, intermingled with the young heroine's burgeoning interest in a normal world that she has never known until now.

Part 2 lacks the focus of the original movie's better-constructed plot, which built up the audience's connection to the first 'witch' protagonist before letting loose with the barbarous battles. I suppose the slow burn nature of *Part 1* would come across as repetitive if repeated here and the big plot twist in *The Witch: Part 1 - The Subversion* couldn't be replicated again. This sequel does have some nicely-sketched characters, though, including the gang boss Yong-du, who is, depending upon his mood, pleasant, vicious, victimised or assertive. At one point he even seems concerned for the girl's safety when he sees her standing on the edge of the roof of Kyung-hee's farmhouse.

The action scenes in this sequel take precedence over the dramatics, and they are certainly hella good and bloody, with the combatants all possessing differing levels of telekinetic and regenerative powers, heightened strength and super-speed. The third act super-scrap, set at the farmhouse with a nearby firework display filling the night sky with sparkling light, is quite a brutal, hyper-powered, often bloody tour de force engagement. People get punched across fields, many, many bullets are fired, combatants slug it out atop a big digital billboard, a character loses an arm and then regrows it, nice characters die, a knife-wielding 'witch' is compelled to repeatedly stab herself, and the main girl protagonist deals with her opponents in a cold, controlled, deadly-but-unemotional manner.

This South Korean sci-fi-action-drama features a compelling opening sequence, where a young pregnant woman (who is carrying twins destined to grow up to be the two heroines of these *Witch* movies) is abducted after everyone else on a bus gets gassed and killed. From then on the movie remains a handsome-looking, crisply shot production that, thanks to the lab-raised super-kid plot, has some *Stranger Things* vibes. It is perhaps a little too convoluted when it comes to keeping track of who all the different warring powered factions are, but it is never less than very entertaining throughout.

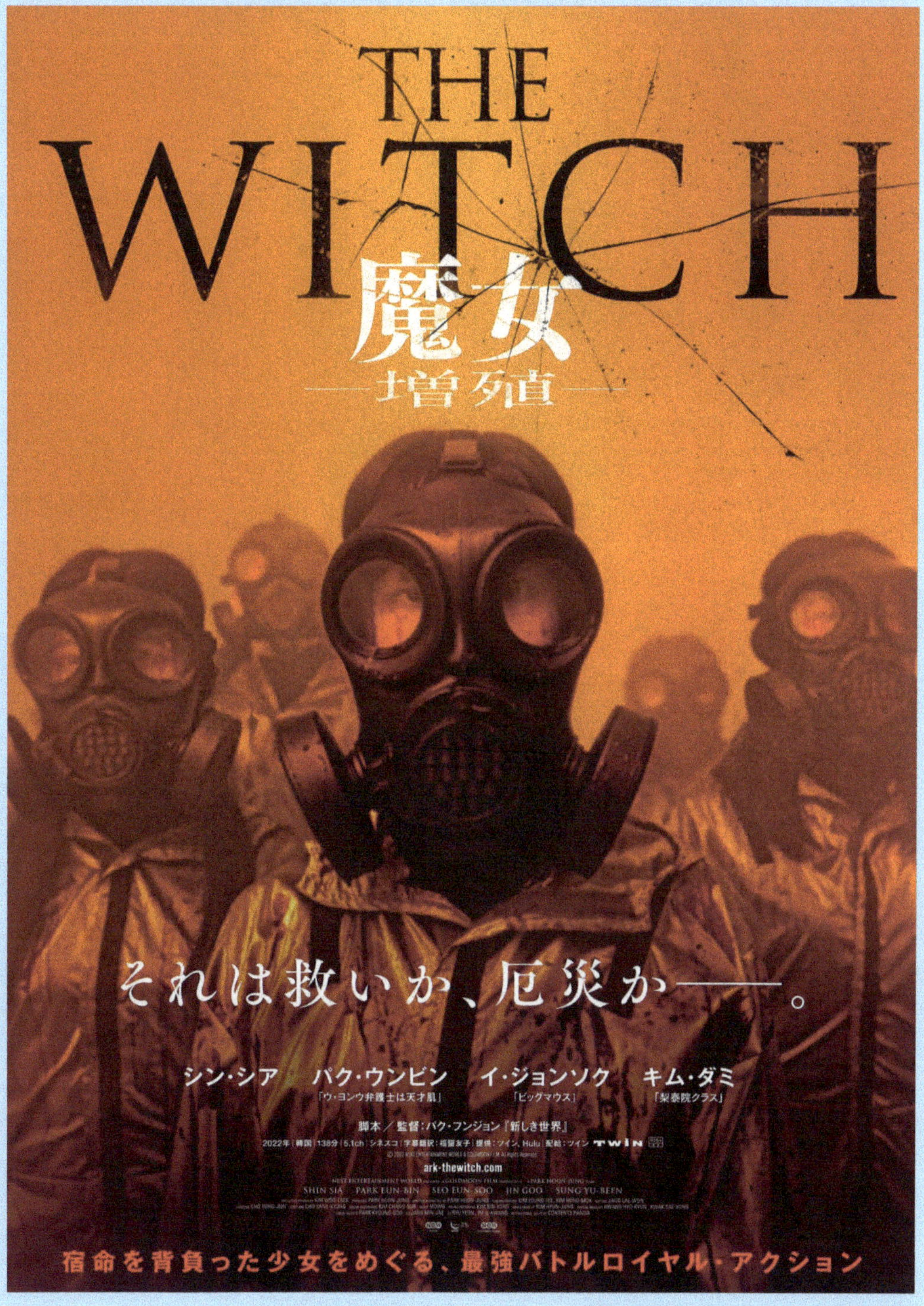

THE RED SPARROW (2022)

Starring Han Congcong, Jiang Zhenhao, Shuxian Zheng
Written by Chen Xi, Liu Zhen
Directed by Ji Zhizhong
Tencent Video

In 2060 a group called the Guardian Angels attempts to thwart the Ron Group, which has plans to rule mankind via the use of implanted chips and AI. The Guardian Angels have created a child who is a merging of humanity and cutting-edge nanotech, born to a woman who has developed a technology referred to as the Phoenix System. But when the Ron Group attacks en masse, the baby, named Yi Ni, has to be launched away from the invaded Guardian Angels base in an escape pod. Twenty years later, Yi Ni (Han Congcong) is a street-smart dealer in liquid metal (and owner of an insufferable little pet robot called Migu), who is living in a vast megalopolis, unaware of her past, but she will soon become instrumental in the renewed conflict between the Ron Group and the remnants of the Guardian Angels...

This Chinese sci-fi-actioner begins with a computer game-like large scale battle set piece between warring forces using auto cannons, missile batteries, future tech aircraft and war-bots against each other, but it's all brought to life with CGI that's far from top shelf quality.

Jumping forward in time, the movie introduces us to the world in which the sassy adult Yi Ni is living in: a *Blade Runner* cityscape crammed with the usual skyscraper-sized holograms, flying cars and *Tron*-esque elevated trackways, but all done with really

Don't worry, that irritating mini robot gets fragged before the movie ends!

low-rent effects. Yi Ni is captured by the Ron Group, which plans to use her DNA to offer 'smart evolution' pharmaceutical breakthroughs to its customers, though this is all a cover for the group's corporate leader, Mr Ron, to embark on his plan to replace mankind with nanobot-controlled automatons (well, I think that's his plan!) You see, Mr Ron is actually a self-aware robot constructed from masses of nanobots that were created from the original Mr Ron's genes (or something like that!) However, the 'Phoenix 2.0' protocol within Yi Ni is activated and she becomes enhanced with nano-upgraded capabilities, and she's saved by a team of Guardian Angels led by Giu De (Zhenhao), who whisk her away from the Ron Group's clutches, though many of them die in the process.

The Red Sparrow has delusions of grandeur, doing its best to come across as a mix of *Blade Runner* (1982) and *Ghost in the Shell* (2017), but its aspirations are constrained by the naff digital effects, which are of the sort that give so many modern Chinese SF/fantasy movies a bad name. Other recent, similar mainland Chinese movies like *Mutant Ghost Wargirl* (2022) actually delivered really pretty decent special effects, but *The Red Sparrow* fails majorly to do the same (even though its promo art really tries to suggest otherwise). But, y'know, there are always some things to like in any given movie, and here we have a brisk training montage sequence, a vampy female villainess (Zheng) and an okay race against time (to shut down an army of robo-warriors before they are activated) to keep viewers occupied.

With a bigger budget and better FX, the final fight with the robo-villain Mr Ron (not a scary name!) would've been a way-cool sequence. As it is, it's all a bit cheap-looking, but then… Mr Ron gets blown up by a rocket launcher and he immediately returns as a vast, spike-limbed, scorpion-tailed spider-droid monster! Irritating 'cute' robo-pet Migu gets vaporised (yay!) by this spider-bot's laser, upsetting Yi Ni and triggering an internal transformation within her. She now becomes a souped-up she-warrior, as rock guitars play on the soundtrack, leaving a trail of virtual flames behind her as she marches straight at the arachnoid! Yi Ni overpowers the spider-thing's nanobot infrastructure, causing it to become semi-molten, then she hovers above it, and, as flaming 'fire-wings' sprout from her back, she blasts the boss-monster to smithereens! Well, this is a pretty silly-fun-cool way to end the movie, forcing me to begrudgingly admit that I rather enjoyed the finale!

KNUCKLE GIRL (2023)

Starring Ayaka Miyoshi, Gouki Maeda, Hideaki Itô, Yosuke Kubozuka, Masaki Miura
Written by Kap Yeol Yu
Directed by Chang
Produced by Steven Nam
Robot Communications Inc.

Feisty boxer Ran (Miyoshi) volunteers to take part in a deathmatch run by a sinister organisation in order to locate her missing sister, Yuzuki. After training and getting boxing advice from her boy-pal Shun (Maeda), Ran enters the underground arena, known as the Garage, to battle man-mountain adversary Kito, armed only with brass knuckles to even the odds. Meanwhile, good cop Suzuki (Miura) sneaks into the server room to attain evidence to take the organisation down, but people are willing to kill and frame Ran for multiple murders…

Based on a Korean Webtoon by Sangjin Yoo and Sangyoung Jun, *Knuckle Girl* is a Japanese/South Korean production that's nice lookin', boasts a well-designed arena set, and features Hideaki Itô as smart, sleek gang boss Haruki Nikaido, who exudes charismatic, amoral villainy from every pore.

The plot isn't particularly original, though it does introduce a cool reason explaining why Yuzuki was kidnapped: she possesses 'golden blood', a rare blood type that Nikaido uses as a super-secure way to maintain a one-off biometric authentication program protecting a gangland fortune.

This film could've been a real cult favourite if more had been made of Ran dealing out bumps and bruises to baddies with her brass knuckles, but she actually only uses them in one arena fight and during the climax. With that said, *Knuckle Girl* is a solid little female fighter flick drama that introduces us to a bunch of likeable protagonists.

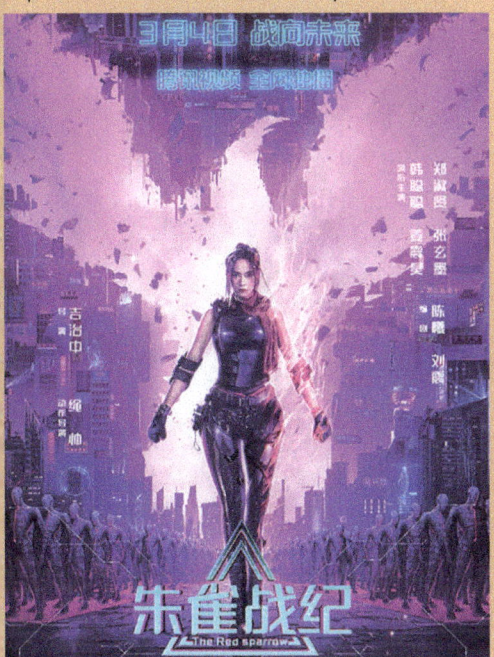

It's a huge spider-bot!

PROJECT WOLF HUNTING (2022)

Starring Seo In-guk, Jang Dong-yoon, Choi Gwi-hwa, Sung Dong-il, Park Ho-san, Jung Moon-sung, Jung So-min
Written by Kim Hong-sun
Directed by Kim Hong-sun
Produced by Gu Seong-mok
Cheum Film/Contents G

A group of South Korean prisoners are transported from the Philippines in the cargo ship Frontier Titan, overseen by a large team of Korean police officers, led by Seok-woo (Ho-san). The surly cons are kept in line by the cops, but it all gets very bloody as a murderous team takes over the vessel, the prisoners are freed, and then an unstoppable being escapes from his restraints in the bowels of the ship...

The start of this South Korean film is paced nicely, showing us around the ship and introducing the cops, the cons and the ship's crew members. But soon the killings start and we're left in no doubt that director Kim Hong-sun intends to deliver a non-stop, blood-drenched, action-filled movie where the visceral, violent aspects of the story take precedence over the plotting and characterisations. This approach has been criticised by some reviewers, but I appreciate Hong-sun's commitment to making such a no-holds-barred production, where the visceral carnage and action is the whole point of the movie. And, anyway, this isn't to say that the characters are blandly sketched, because the director still manages to imbue many of the bad guys with a warped, sick charisma, especially the tattooed psycho Jong-du (In-guk) and the ruthless, machine gun-toting inside man Kim (Moon-sung).

When the superhuman killing machine Alpha (Gwi-hwa) begins his murder spree at the midpoint, the carnage intensifies. Alpha, who has swollen flesh around his eyes that are sewn shut with outsized staples, stomps loudly about the ship like a part-zombie terminator. This monstrous dude cannot be reasoned with and is revealed to be a lobotomised human weapon test subject from the Kemono Project, a Japanese-run experiment dating back to the Second World War. We're even treated to a flashback that shows Alpha bludgeoning a team of Japanese soldiers to death with a human skull!

An extra layer of complication is added for the surviving cops (and several 'nice' cons) when it's divulged that the pharma company Aeon Genetics is behind the presence of Alpha on the ship: they'd been bringing Alpha to South Korea to find out why he doesn't age. With chaos reigning on the cargo vessel, Aeon flies in a helicopter full of mercs, but these die in grisly ways, just like most of the cast.

In a film where various characters are revealed to be the super-powered results of experimentation, arterial blood-jets go off like lawn sprinklers, and heads get caved-in on a regular basis, this well-shot, ultra-violent sci-fi-horror-actioner keeps you constantly guessing as to which characters might stand a chance of surviving until the end of a movie that's awash with puddles, squirts, rivulets and torrents of blood!

I really enjoyed this one!

IN MY MOTHER'S SKIN (2023)

Starring Felicity Kyle Napuli, Angeli Bayani, Jasmine Curtis-Smith, James Mavie Estrella, Beauty Gonzalez, Shion Hayakawa
Written by Kenneth Dagatan
Directed by Kenneth Dagatan
Produced by Bianca Balbuena, Stefano Centini, Junxiang Huang
Epicmedia Productions/Clover Films/Volos Films Co/Zhao Wei Films

During the Second World War in the Japanese-occupied Philippines, a well-off merchant, who is accused of hiding a stash of gold, decides to seek help, leaving his wife, daughter and son to fend for themselves in their large, isolated home. The daughter, Tala (Felicity Kyle Napuli), encounters a 'cicada fairy' (Jasmine Curtis-Smith) dwelling in a derelict, chapel-like jungle shack. This fairy persuades Tala to allow a cicada to crawl into her ill mother's mouth, which seems to heal her at first, but a large, fleshy cyst develops on the mother's back... and soon she begins to lose her humanity, eats the pet dog, and pleads to be locked up so that she can't harm her children. Tala realises that the seemingly friendly fairy can not be trusted, but when her brother, Bayani (James Mavie Estrella), then accidentally shoots himself in the stomach, she's forced to return to the fairy's hut-chapel to plead for help again...

In My Mother's Skin, a Philippines/Singapore/Taiwan production, has a persuasive aura of doom, that is accentuated by the movie's score. Catholic imagery abounds, with the family home full of statues and other Christian iconography. The cicada fairy, interestingly, resembles a fantastical parody of the Catholic concept of the

Virgin Mary. Her striking, gilded, gaudy costume has a headdress resembling a fan of sparkly insect wings, and she at first comes across as benign and helpful when Tala meets her in the wooden shack in the forest, which has stained glass windows featuring images of 'angels' with insect wings.

The film is like a Filipino Guillermo del Toro production, mixing fantasy fairy tale elements with horror. The horrific aspects of the film include the mother becoming a long-tongued, veiny-faced cannibal. Tala uses her animalistic mother to deal with a violent would-be robber at one point, telling the man he can find the hidden, stolen gold in her mother's bedroom. This crook, of course, gets killed and munched on by the mom. A fantastical component of the tale involves a golden, glowing fruit that the 'friendly' fairy instructs Tala to eat. Tala refuses to do this, and horror comes to the fore again as soon as Tala returns to her home, finding Bayani's severed head lying on the floor and her monstrous mother waiting to attack her.

Memorable moments include the fairy biting off the head of a bird, and glimpses of the youthful-looking fairy's true, wizened visage.

It all ends depressingly, with the newly returned father hugging his son's severed head and crying, as the movie strives to appear deeper and more meaningful than it actually is, though *In My Mother's Skin* definitely possesses some rather striking imagery, with the 'fairy' character proving to be, without a doubt, the film's most interesting element.

SAKRA (2023)

Starring Donnie Yen, Wu Yue, Chen Yuqi, Cya Liu, Wai Ying Hung
Written by Sheng Lingzhi, Zhu Wei, He Ben
Directed by Donnie Yen
Produced by Donnie Yen, Wong Jing
Plus Entertainment/Wishart Media

In Song Dynasty China, when the country was at war with the Khitans, the martial arts super-master Qiao Feng (Yen), leader of the Beggars Gang, is framed for the murders of his adoptive parents and his master, is revealed to be of Khitan origin, and is forced to fight off attacks from his former colleagues as he seeks to discover the identity of the person who set him up.

Based on part of Louis Cha's wuxia novel *Demi-Gods and Semi Devils*, this Hong Kong/Chinese production details Qiao Feng's quest to discover the secrets of his past and hunt down the mysterious 'leading brother' responsible for the murders of his parents. With a large cast of characters, including Azhu (Yuqi), who is the lover of Qiao Feng, the plot can be convoluted, with various deceptions and devious alliances to keep track of, so the film really needed a sure hand to guide the tale, but Yen's storytelling skills aren't his strong point here, unfortunately, which leaves us struggling sometimes to follow certain plot points. Fortunately, Yen, along with co-director Kam Ka Wai, makes up for the story shortcomings with the full-on, entertaining action set pieces. Though the fights occasionally look too speeded up, the fast, frenetic nature of the combat scenes, which incorporate loads of kinetic, hectic wirework, are a great deal of fun to watch.

In the fantasy-fu world of this movie, the righteous, stoic, stern hero Qiao Feng possesses super-powered skills: he can snatch handfuls of arrows from the air, leap great distances, punch horses to the ground, create swirling wind vortexes, and can defeat enemies using concussive shockwaves. Other characters boast equally enhanced abilities, as they control flames with their hands, bound from rooftop to rooftop, or utilise *Mission Impossible*-style masks for disguise.

Sakra is a handsome-looking production with good sets and costumes, but its main asset is definitely the action, courtesy of action directors Kenji Tanigaki, Yan Hua, Zhang Chao and Donnie Yen's Action Team, which treats us to over the top face-offs that feature one-against-many brawls, fighters getting punched through walls and roofs, and skirmishes in which the opponents are able to manipulate the air around them.

VEERAN (2023)

Starring Hiphop Tamizha Adhi, Athira Raj, Sassi Selvaraj, Vinay Rai
Written by Ark Saravan
Directed by Ark Saravan
Produced by Arjun Thyagarajan, Sendhil Thyagarajan
Sathya Jyothi Films

A boy called Kumaran (Adhi) is struck by lightning when passing by the local village shrine to the god Veeran. He is sent abroad for medical care and doesn't return for a few years. When Kumaran does come back home he discovers that Selvi (Raj), the girl he was very close with, is about to get married. He also finds himself standing up to a corporation that intends to run a dangerous power cable through the village, requiring the demolition of the Veeran shrine. Kumaran takes on the guise of the god Veeran, becoming a fighter for justice, and he is able to convince those around him that he is a powerful being because he really does have electrical superpowers!

Helped by his former school friends, Kumaran rides around on a horse, zaps villains, uses his electrical energy to mind-control people, and eventually helps to defeat the corporate baddies.

Veeran, a Tamil language Indian film, presents us with likeable characters and some entertaining situations. Adhi, a Tamil hip hop star, is okay, in a low-key, restrained way, as the reluctant hero Kumaran, who wears a robe-like costume when pretending to be Veeran. The two Bollywood song and

dance numbers incorporated into the film are not obtrusive and are good-natured little musical interludes, and, generally, the movie is an easy-going affair.

Unfortunately, the screenplay is very lazily written. The storyline involving Selvi's imminent marriage gets forgotten, then is featured again, then gets dropped once more. Kumaran is a very reactive character much of the time, not using his powers in scenes when it made sense for him to do so (such as when village prisoners are getting slapped around). Ark Saravan, who wrote and directed the film, really should have shaped this project into a leaner, far more focused form. Instead, he haphazardly fills the running time with 'funny' secondary characters and too many pointless scenes. The company power cable scheme is never really explained, and neither is the top villain's penchant for making people erupt into green gunk.

Worth watching once, though, if you have some time on your hands. ●

> "When I was little, my father was famous. He was the greatest samurai in the empire, and he was the Shogun's decapitator."
>
> Voice of Daigorō

SHOGUN ASSASSIN INTERVIEW

VOICE OF THE WOLF CUB

GIBRAN EVANS

INTERVIEWED BY SIMON PRITCHARD AND KEN MILLER

In *Shogun Assassin* the hero's young son, Daigorō, is the storyteller, his voiceover used to connect all the re-edited footage together, helping immeasurably with the overall flow of the tale. This decision to use Lone Wolf's Cub as the central narrator was a masterstroke, utilising the innocent-but-world-weary childish vocals of the boy to infuse the film with a truly distinctive tone. Daigorō was played by Akihiro Tomikawa, but it was an American youngster, **Gibran Evans**, who provided the Cub with his characteristic voice in *Shogun Assassin*...

How old were you when you did the voice work for Daigorō in *Shogun Assassin*?

I was 7 years old when the recording took place in 1980, living in Malibu at the time with my father, brother and two dogs.

What was the background to you becoming involved in the project?

My father was creating the poster art along with the title logo for the film and was a close colleague and friends with the producer David Weisman and director Bobby Houston.

Did it take long to record the voice tracks?

The entire process took one afternoon at a sound studio next door to the old Hollywood Storage Company Building at 1025 Highland Avenue.

I have fond memories of the giant Bekins Storage sign painted on the building's side, during those years of being shuttled around Hollywood while my father worked.

Gibran is now a top design creative

Did you have any influence or were there any changes to the script once you started to record it?

I had no direct influence, I was 7 and barely understood what the context was of anything I was recording.

However, I do recall some alternate takes due to getting tongue twisted by some lines that were too long or too

A Polaroid shot of Gibran from when he was a youngster...

"Then, one night, the Shogun sent his ninja spies to our house. They were supposed to kill my father, but they didn't. That was the night everything changed, forever. That was when my father left his samurai life and became a demon..."

Film Frenzy Page 50

complex, which forced them to adjust on my behalf.

Were you shown footage from this movie when you were dubbing it? It's very violent and bloody!

I was not shown the footage prior or during the recording but did see it shortly after release when I was 8. The violence was almost fantasy-like and the film so culturally obscure that it didn't really frighten me.

The only violence that really stuck with me was the guy hiding under the sand getting clawed on the top of the head - it looked painful and lasted a while, whilst many other incidents were quick and precise. The guy getting all of his limbs sliced off for sport/demonstration by the Supreme Ninja seemed a bit mean-spirited and I also found that a little distressing.

Shogun Assassin was a US movie created by editing together footage from the Japanese films *Lone Wolf and Cub: Sword of Vengeance* (1972) and *Lone Wolf and Cub: Baby Cart at the River Styx* (1972), with a new soundtrack and dubbed English voices added. But *Shogun Assassin*

You better not mess with the Supreme Ninja!

This dude likes to claw people's heads!

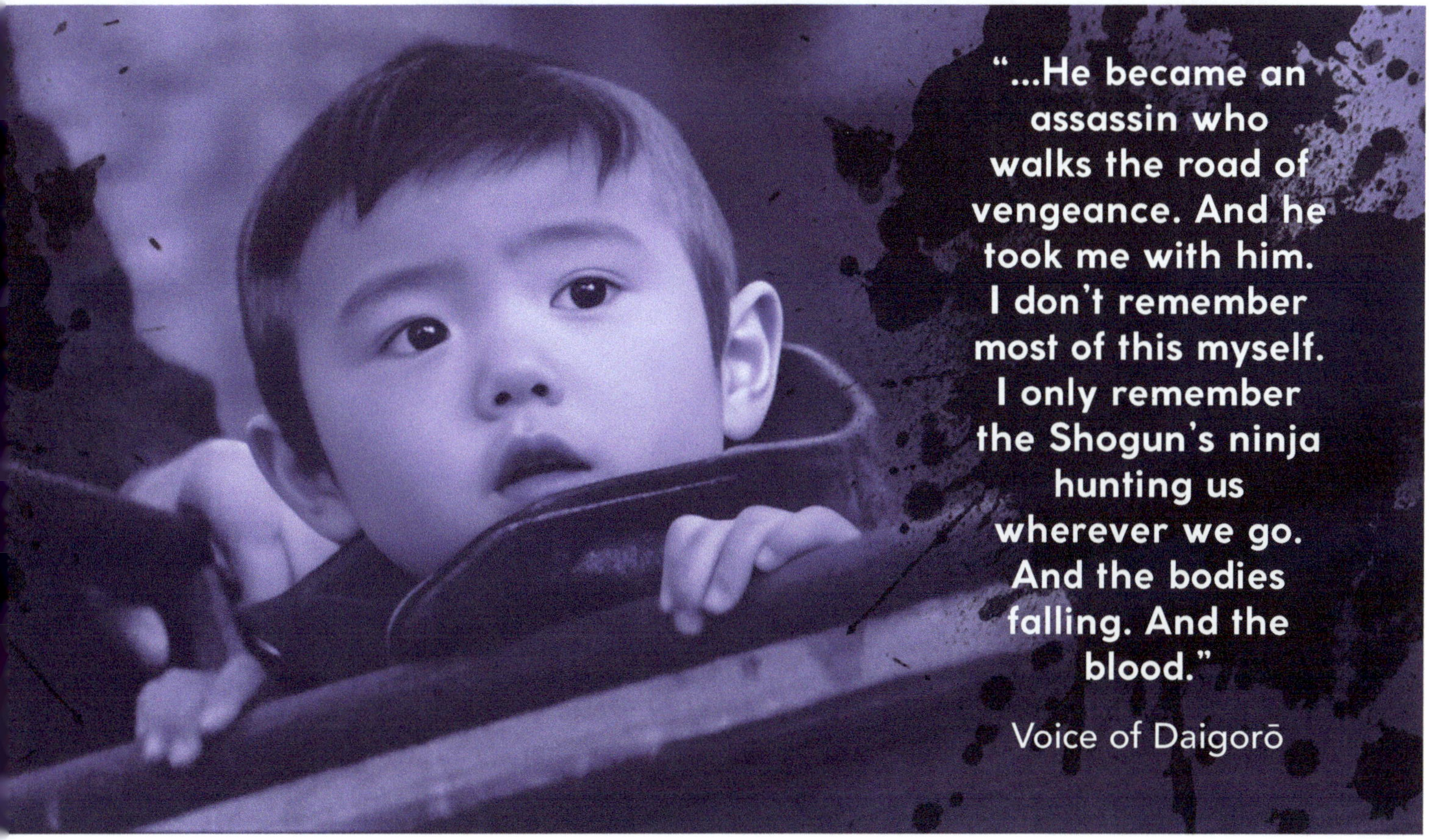

"...He became an assassin who walks the road of vengeance. And he took me with him. I don't remember most of this myself. I only remember the Shogun's ninja hunting us wherever we go. And the bodies falling. And the blood."

Voice of Daigorō

transcended its origins to become a well-liked movie in its own right. What do you think has helped it to become such a long-lasting cult favourite?

As far as I know there wasn't a lot of this kind of cinema available in the US unless you knew where to look. In retrospect, even as early as 10 years later, the music, my voice, the premise of the father & child, the quite elegant directing, the editing and voiceover/writing turned it into a unique, well crafted film by any standards, and it had no choice but to become a timeless classic.

You provided an audio commentary for *Shogun Assassin* on the Eureka Entertainment Blu-ray release. What was this like to revisit the film in such depth and what memories did this bring back?

In 2010 I had gotten the request via my father by way of David Weisman. I was terrified and very nervous at the prospect of being recorded for something I hadn't thought about since *Liquid Swords* was released in 1995, 15 years earlier, and 15 years prior to that when I recorded it. I didn't really feel like I had much to contribute - David was the main point on that interview, and I felt a bit more of a decorative appearance. However, a woman named Carmen who worked at the studio doing the recording, seemed to be oddly excited about my presence, and it turned out she was a huge fan. I was shocked to meet anyone this excited about me or my childhood voice, and it was only shortly after I learned that GZA was still performing *Liquid Swords* and thousands of people were reciting my voice at concerts.

What are your favourite scenes from the film?

The whole sequence of the Supreme Ninja and her minions with their three-tiered attack on the road: I thought it was cool how they hid knives in their radishes, and Daigorō got to use his spring-loaded front blade, and got his ponytail sliced off by a flying hat.

What do you remember about the time *Shogun Assassin* was originally released?

Not much really, I think I saw it on VHS at home for the first time under the context of... 'here is that thing you did'.

Your voiceover narration is a central, memorable component of the film's appeal. How did you create the tone in your voice that exudes that famous 'sombre/innocent finality'?

I was a quiet kid, spending a lot of time in nature, I was generally polite and soft spoken. I think the music really helps the tone, but this is pretty

"When we're on a mission, I keep count of how many ninja my father kills. He says not to keep count, only to pray for their souls. But if I don't keep count, I don't know how many souls to pray for. So I keep count. So far it's three hundred and forty-two."

Voice of Daigorō

much how I sounded without much effort at the time.
The lines were spoken to me first, which I believe led to a slow, thoughtful recitation/presentation on my part, which comes out. The only major direction I recall was whenever the word 'Shogun' came up, that I should try to say it with a deeper voice and hold the 'O' for emphasis, neither of which I feel I really achieved, but I was making a mindful effort at the time.

Shogun Assassin became a cult film and was included on the British Board of Classification's original "banned" list of films. Copies were seized and the film was prosecuted for obscenity, but the prosecution failed. It was not until the late 90's that the film was released uncut in the UK. Were you aware of the film's popularity and infamy worldwide after its release? What do you think about this?

I knew it was a cult classic but wasn't aware it was banned or seized till I got my hands on a DVD in the early 2000s that said 'Banned Since 1983' on the cover.
I think I was always about a decade behind knowing how popular this film and my voice had become. It's a bit shocking any movie gets banned, and in the case of *Shogun Assassin* seems like an overreaction.

You did the voice work for *Shogun Assassin*, but never did anything similar in movies afterwards. Were

you ever interested in getting more involved in the movie industry as a performer?

I was thrown into another film in 1984 called Bad Manners as an extra along with my brother, also directed by Bobby Houston. I was not inclined to perform; this was more spearheaded by my father who as I recall was a bit too busy to be running me and my brother around for this kind of work in the centre of his career as a commercial illustrator.

Shogun Assassin has been sampled many times, including by GZA from The Wu-Tang Clan. It must be cool to hear your voice used in albums like Liquid Swords?!

Yeah, it's pretty cool and has definitely got me a bit of cred over the years, a few friends on social media and my first official autograph request which led me to Eastern Heroes. At the time Liquid Swords was released, it was very weird for my voice to seemingly come out of nowhere and most people looked at me in disbelief when I told them it was me.

I remember being in the theatre with my son when they played the bit in Kill Bill 2 and I got all teary-eyed with a warm feeling in my stomach.

Watching Shogun Assassin...

You've been part of your father's TAZ collective and you are a senior creative at the Division 13 Design Group, a creative team that designs & produces posters, websites/social media, games, live events, mailers, digital stickers, video promos, and other branded activations for the entertainment industry. What posters and other movie-related branded activations that you've worked on are you most pleased with?

The large series of TAZ posters from the 90s were a blast and the ever so popular Ill Communication album packaging was pretty fun. I'd say I've

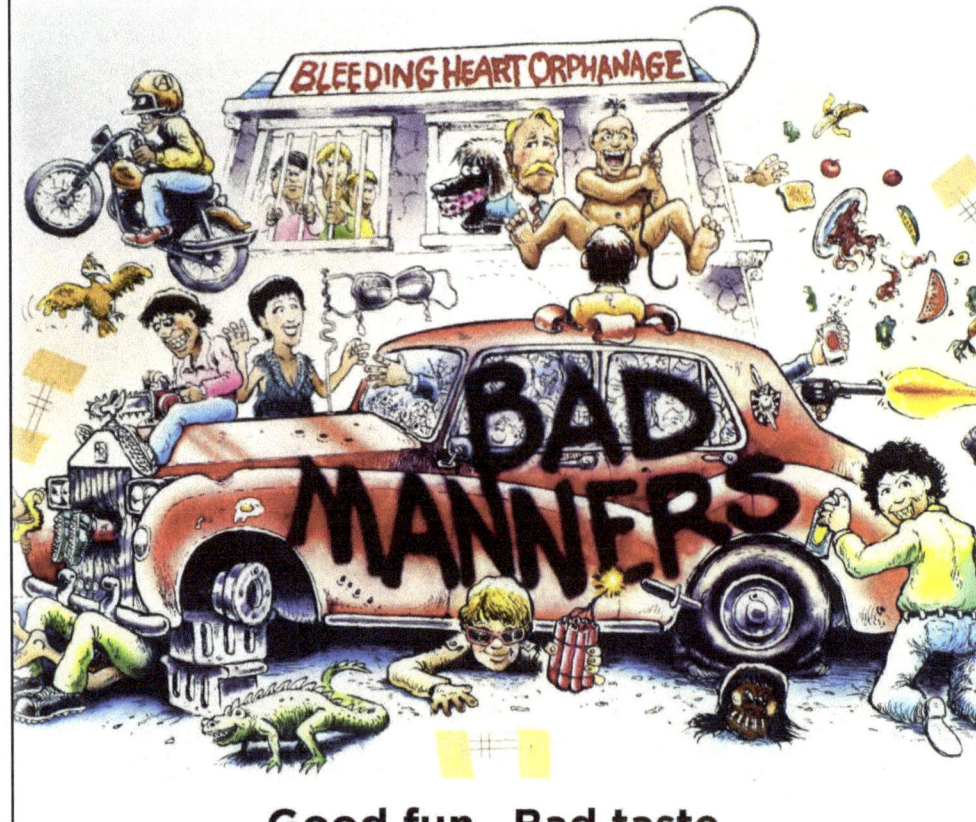

"I guess I wish it was different."

"But a wish is only a wish."

Voice of Daigorō

Gibran's DVD signed by GZA!

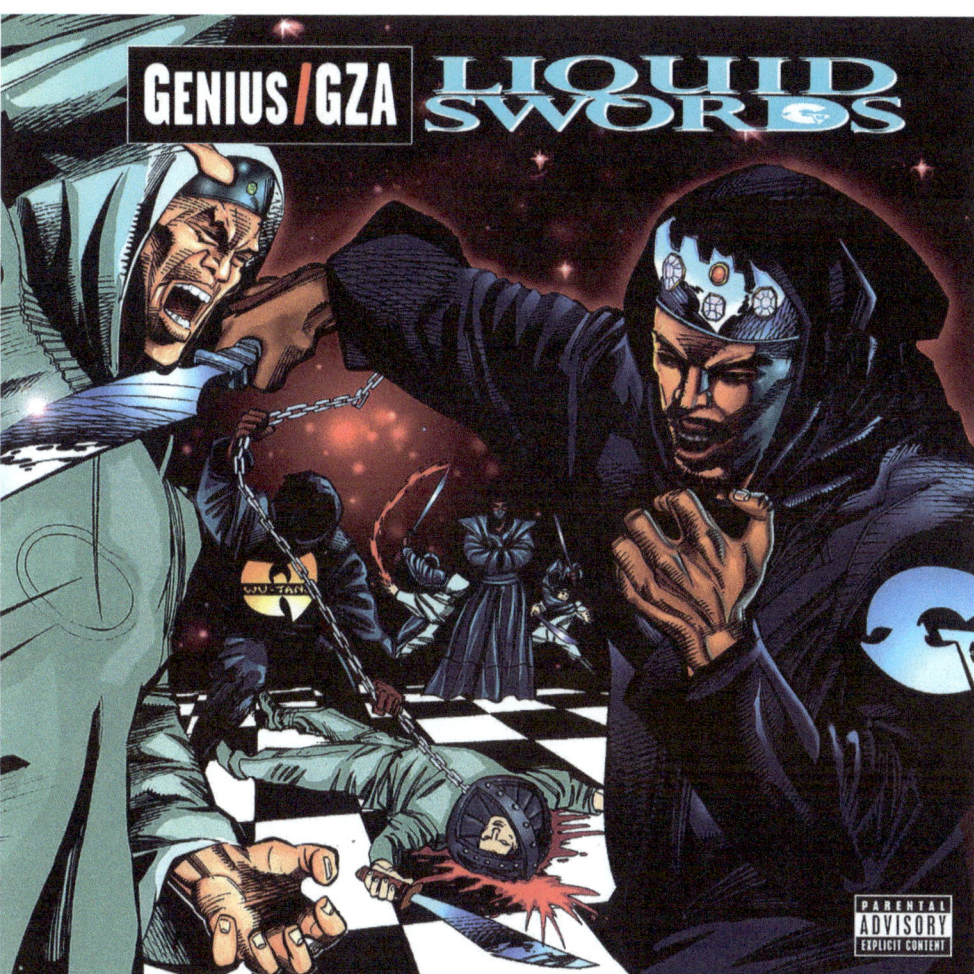

worked on about 400+ major film productions over the last 25-30 years.

Favourite websites I worked on from way back were for *The Big Lebowski*, *The Ring*, and a pile of DreamWorks animation sites such as *Sinbad*, *Madagascar*, *Shark Tale*, *Kung Fu*

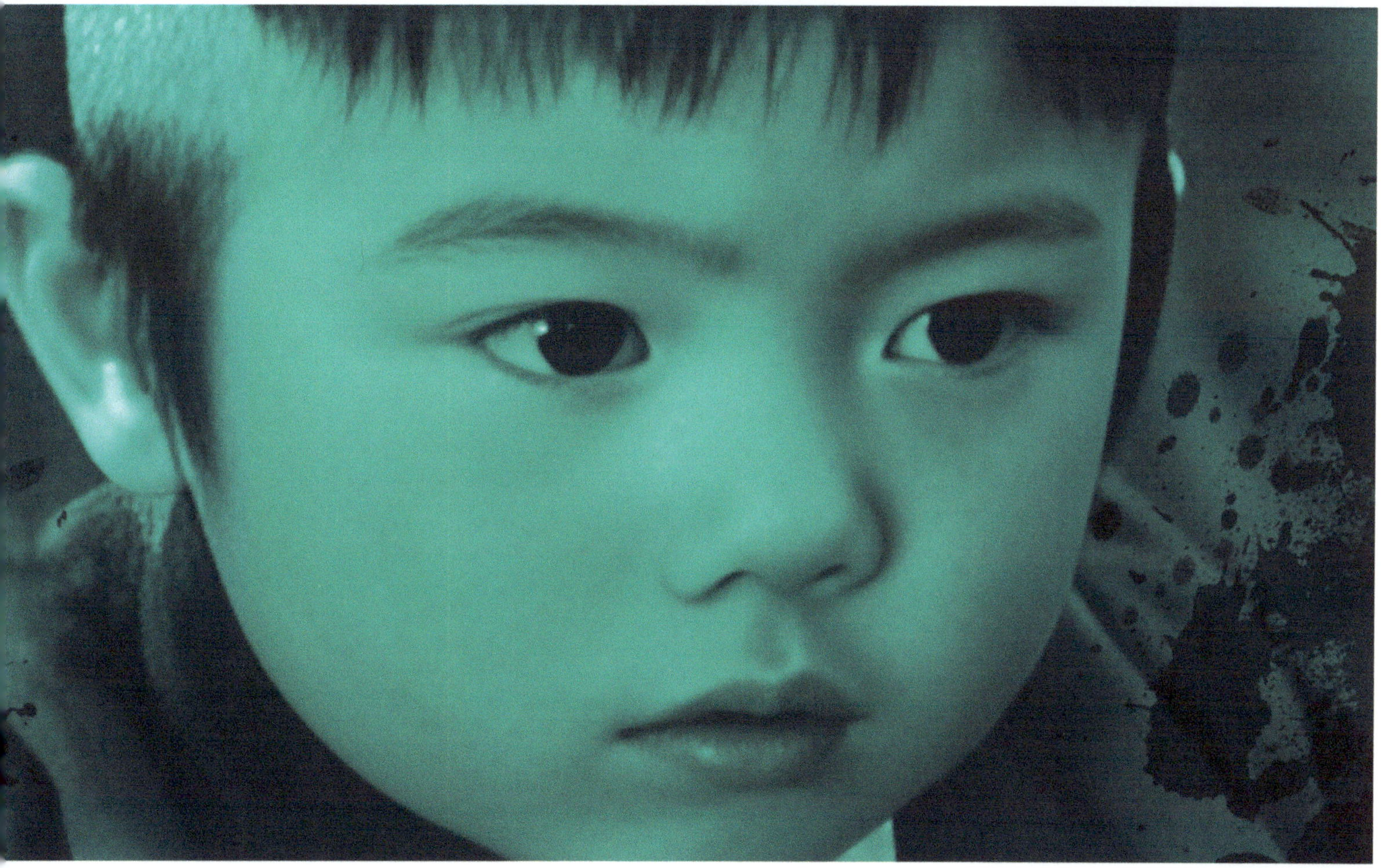

Panda, Monsters vs Aliens, Shrek 3 & Shrek 4, etc... These days things have moved more into ad banners, social media content and mobile games.

Things I'm most proud of usually come with a love of the property, or creative direction, that promotes a deep inspiration, and brings great satisfaction to their executions.

Recent hits were Gran Turismo, Dumb Money, Napoleon, Thanksgiving, 65, and some series work for Outlander, Better Call Saul, Cobra Kai, along with catalogue work doing a huge set of 4k Ultra HD Steel book animated pack shots.

What are your plans for the future and is there any chance fans will ever see you at a Comic Con?

The future regarding little Daigorō... I've been dancing around the idea of directing and animating an interpretive short to run over 'The Legend Of Lone Wolf' (track 1 from the Shogun Assassin film score), which I recently obtained permission to monetise. I love animation, however, to solo something of that scope in my spare time will likely take the better part of a year. Regarding Comic Con, not likely, public appearances aren't really for me.

Thank you for all your time, Gibran. Is there anything else you would like to add, maybe another memory related to your recording session for Shogun Assassin?

During the initial casting call to sample children's voices, they had me sit on a table to reach the mic, and I recall the sound tech getting annoyed at how fidgety I was, swinging my legs back and forth making unnecessary noise. It was my understanding they voice-tested at least a couple hundred options. During the actual recording they put me in a lounge chair and put a pillow under my legs and one under each

ILL COMMUNICATION
BEASTIE BOYS

Gibran collaborated with Adam Yauch to create all the album's packaging. The b&w photograph chosen for the front cover was taken by Magnum photographer Bruce Davidson in 1964 at a Los Angeles drive-in diner. The painting 'Gaia' by Alex Grey was featured in the album's spread. Gibran got his father Jim to draw each letter of the special typeface used for this album, then he scanned them, cleaned it all up in Illustrator, and assembled everything in the font editor Fontographer.

arm to keep me from making noise. The negotiated price for my recording was 200 dollars and as many Famous Amos cookies and all the Coca-Cola I wanted.

One more thing: I went to a concert nearby in January 2023 for a performance of *Liquid Swords* along with a meet & greet ticket for GZA, where I obtained a lovely photo and a signed DVD... The expression on his face when I told him who I was reminded me of all those people with looks of disbelief. His manager on the other hand seemed very excited. 🔵

Gibran meets GZA!

AN ANIMATED DAIGORŌ

This is Gibran's initial character design concept for Daigorō, showing how he would look in the animated short he is planning to make!

Gibran intends to do the concepts and storyboards by hand, the design in Illustrator & Photoshop, and all the animation in After Effects.

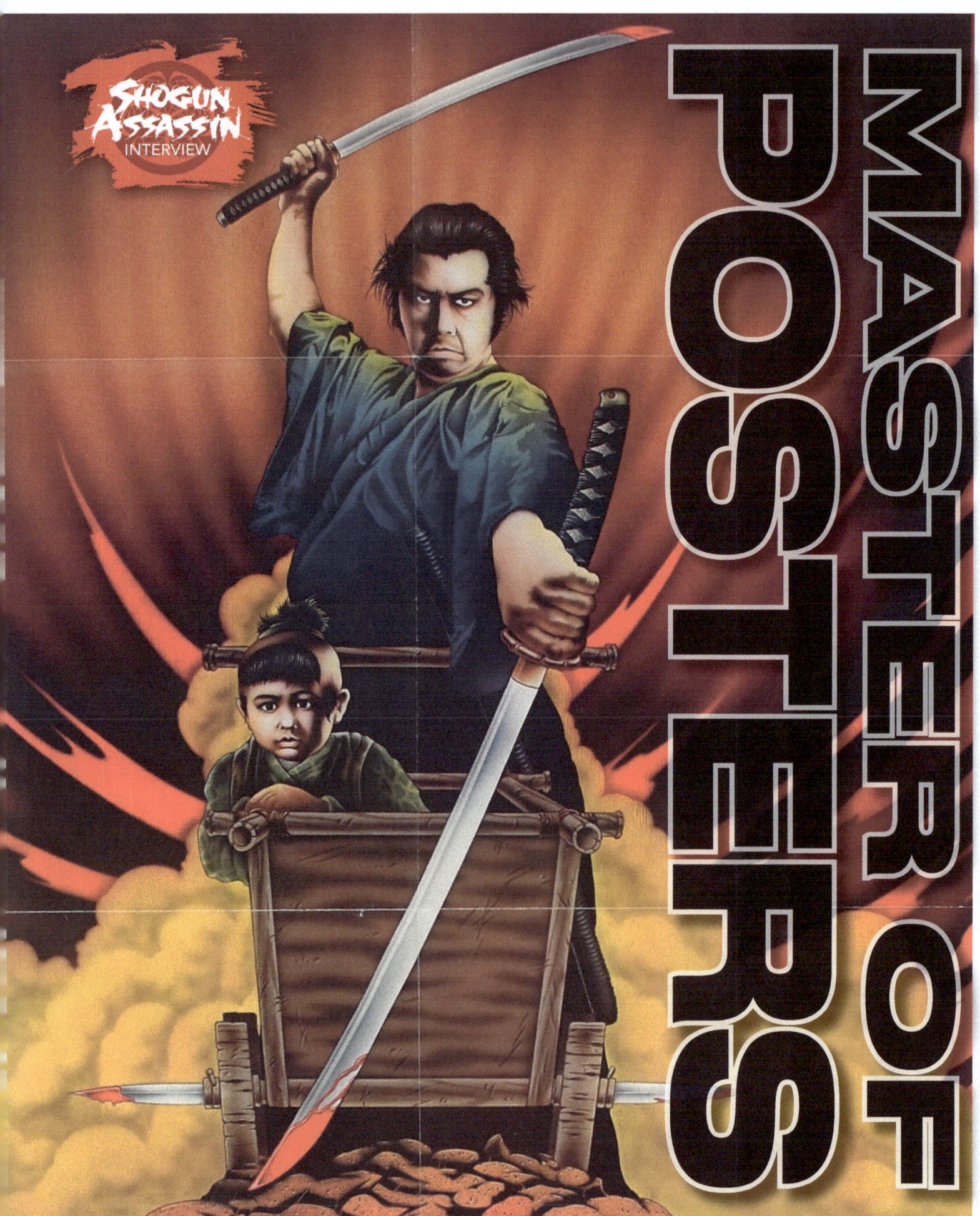

JIM EVANS

INTERVIEWED BY KEN MILLER AND SIMON PRITCHARD

Jim Evans, aka **TAZ**, is a creative renaissance man within the world of commercial art: he has been an Underground Comix artist, a surfing magazine illustrator, a creator of gig posters, record sleeves and rock ephemera for major bands. He has produced many movie posters too, has displayed work at exhibitions, and is the founder of the TAZ collective. Jim was one of the main members of the creative team that brought *Shogun Assassin* into the world, painting the awesome poster and contributing to the film from the outset of the project, influencing all aspects of the graphics and production, helping to develop what ultimately evolved into an iconic piece of pop culture. Here Jim talks about his art, about working on *Shogun Assassin*, describes how he went about painting the legendary poster, and he also reveals an exclusive snippet of information regarding a link between *Shogun Assassin* and a certain Arnold Schwarzenegger movie...

Early in your career you worked as an artist on Underground Comix, on titles like *Yellow Dog*, *Illuminations* and *Slow Death Funnies*. What was it like back then, working within such a heady, countercultural environment?

It was an amazing time to be a young artist. With underground publications in every major city having huge readerships, an artist could gain instant recognition.
This often led to getting a shot at being included in comix like *Yellow Dog*, etc. and eventually getting your own title. Doing covers was always cool, because you got to work in full colour.

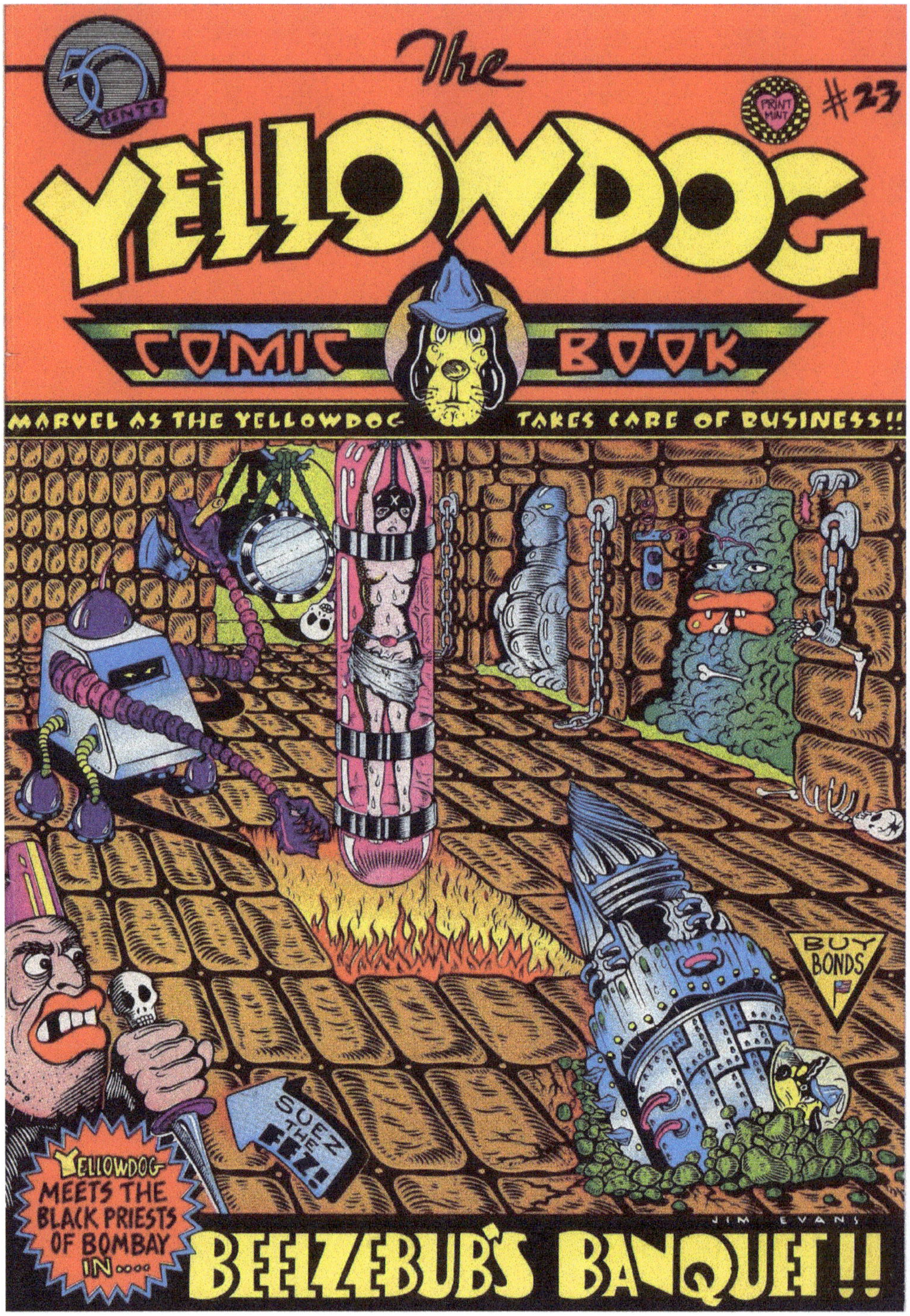

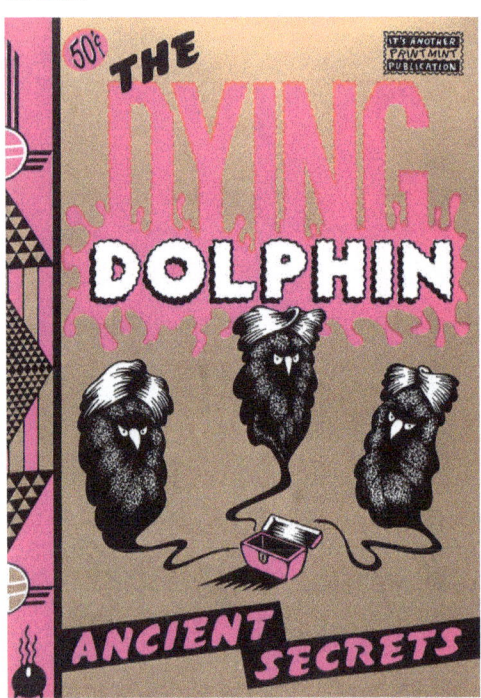

Did you meet-up with other renowned Underground Comix creators at the time, folks such as Robert Crumb, Gilbert Shelton and Richard Corben?

I did meet all of them, except for Richard Corben. I was close friends with Rick Griffin and Robert Williams and did cartoon jam-session collaborations with both of them. Rick, along with Ron Cobb, was key to kick-starting my career, and got me introductions to major publishers like the Print Mint. Rick, myself, Robert Williams, S. Clay Wilson, and Robert Crumb all contributed to *Tales From The Tube*, a comic that was published by *Surfer Magazine*, then later expanded and republished by the Print Mint.

You moved to Hawaii, where you contributed to surfing mags and you illustrated surfing posters. Did you move to Hawaii specifically because you were a surfer and such a big surfing fan?

I planned to move my family to Australia and live a more off-the-grid lifestyle. Being an obsessed surfer, I wanted to take some time in Hawaii and try my hand at giant waves on the North Shore of Oahu. I started getting lots of work in Hawaii and realised I'd disappear in Australia,

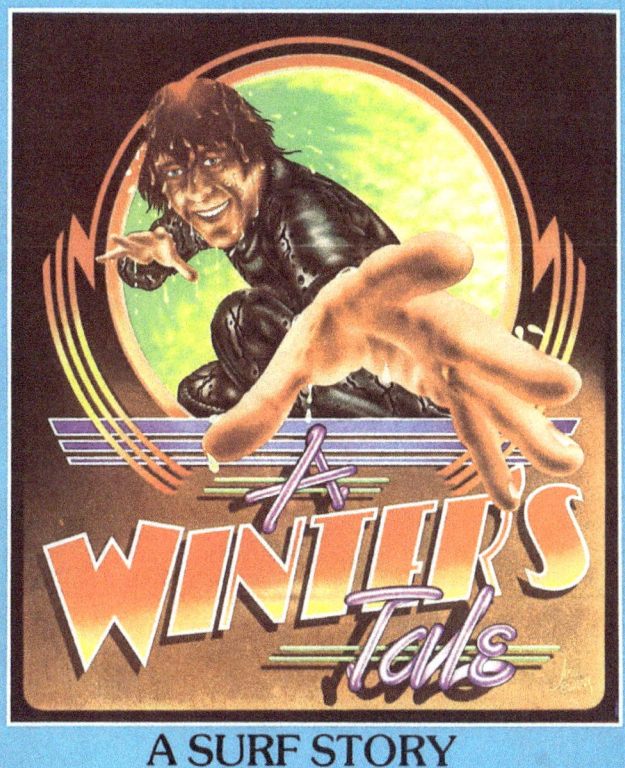

so came back to the mainland after a few years and started getting big album covers, film posters, and a lot of advertising work. My off-the-grid plan did not work out.

You returned to mainland America and did a lot of album sleeve work, for bands including The Beach Boys and Chicago, plus skateboarding magazine illustrations. Was your move from Comix, to surf mags, to album art and skateboard mags always an intentional decision, or did the shift into these different creative areas happen organically?

The shift happened organically; the jobs just kept getting bigger.

Fortunately, I was not an artist who was tied to any medium or movement. For me, the comics were an entry level thing, a way to showcase my ideas and techniques. I had a ton of ideas, and pretty much embraced every new challenge. The album covers and magazine illustrations also entailed more collaboration, and the responsibility to visualise something that was not generated by me, like a band's music and the band's need for a unique and iconic image that represented how they saw themselves.

You started creating movie poster illustrations for films such as 20th Century Oz and Rust Never Sleeps, and you were also a storyboard artist. What movies did you produce storyboards for?

Yes, I did a lot of film posters, and I still do them now for films like

Zombieland 2, *Jumanji*, *Jigsaw*, etc. I did the storyboards for a film titled *Bad Manners*, and another titled *Strangers Kiss*.

My son Gibran, the voice of Daigorō in *Shogun Assassin*, also appears in *Bad Manners*, along with his brother Tagore. Some of the same production team was involved, and the director Robert Houston was the co-director of *Shogun Assassin*. He later went on the win an Academy Award for a documentary film.

How did you become involved with the *Shogun Assassin* project?

I did a lot of genre film posters for the producer, David Weisman, and one day he said that he wanted to create some sort of ultimate Samurai film for domestic US consumption. He asked me what my favourite Samurai film was and I told him a series titled *Lone Wolf and Cub* aka *Baby Cart* was next level cool – that is how it began.

I took him to see an episode at a theatre in Little Tokyo and he agreed immediately that this was the one. David spoke fluent Japanese, and was able to get on the phone and kick the project into gear very quickly.

How was it decided to release a mix between the first two Japanese *Baby Cart* movies rather than just re-releasing them as original 'stand alone' versions?

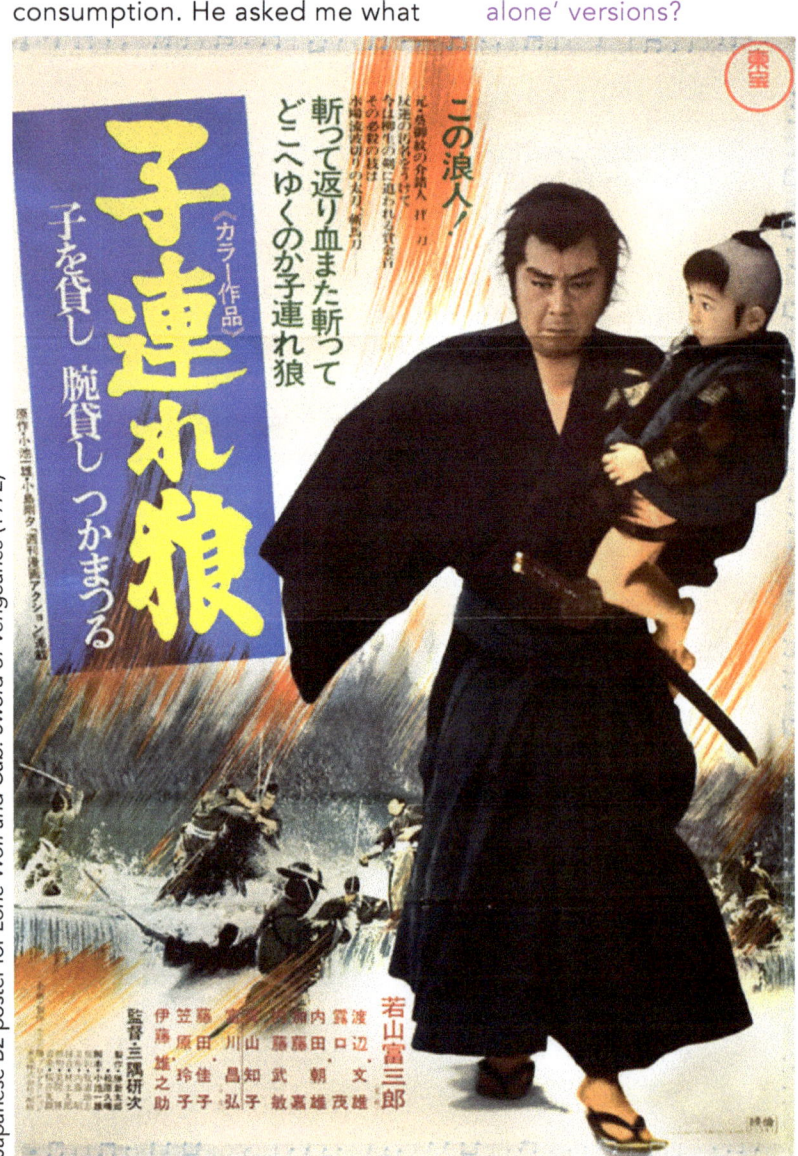

Japanese B2 poster for *Lone Wolf and Cub: Sword of Vengeance* (1972)

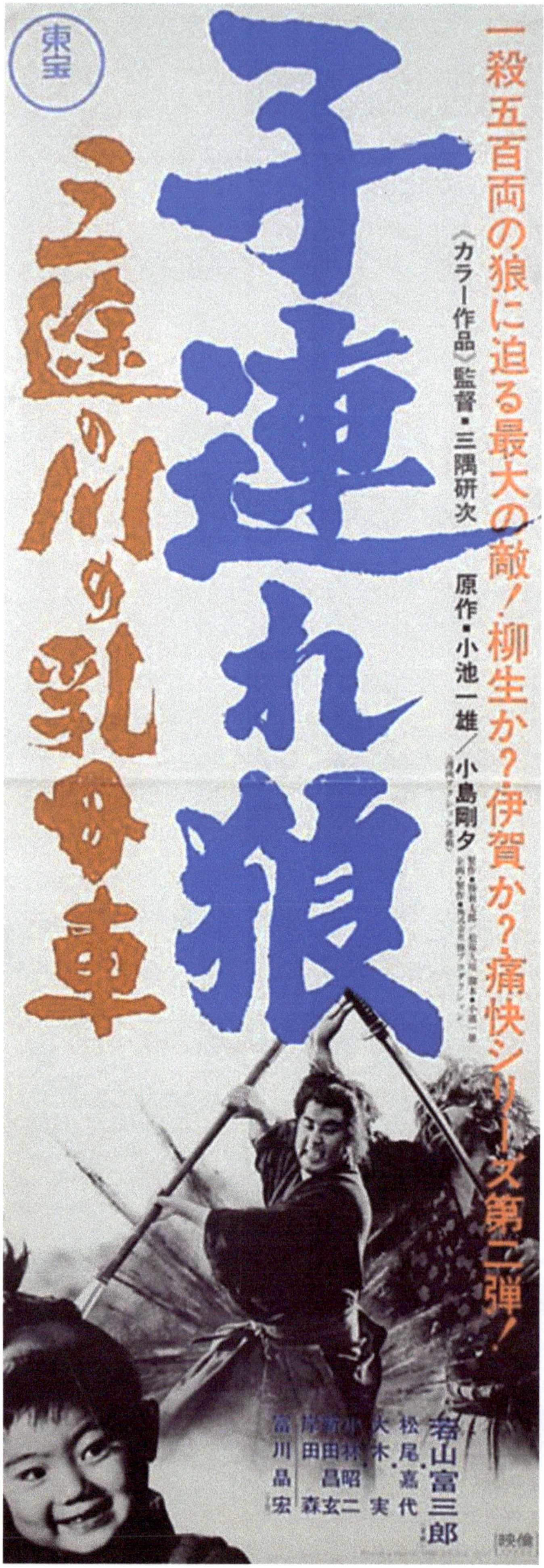

Japanese insert poster for *Lone Wolf and Cub: Baby Cart at the River Styx* (1972): Jim already knew about these Baby Cart movies and encouraged producer David Weisman to purchase the rights

They wanted to redo it completely, and the first two episodes provided the best way to do that.

The team behind it had talented scriptwriters and some seasoned filmmakers. They wanted to showcase the genesis of Ogami Ittō's journey, and why he had taken his young son on such a merciless path of vengeance. Now the original *Shogun Assassin*, if released, would likely become the first part of a trilogy.

Do you remember anything about when or how the decision was made to take the first twelve minutes of *Sword of Vengeance* and use the majority of *Baby Cart at the River Styx* to create the film?

I think once the decision was made to give the child a voice and make him the narrator, all the thoughts about what footage to use was based on that. The first two episodes fit the bill, and the idea was to use the child's voice as a poetic counterpoint to the brutal violence.

The voice of Daigorō has become the most memorable part of *Shogun Assassin*, and the iconic juxtaposition of the sword or the ball is a classic meme.

There may have been rights issues at play as to how much footage could be used, and I remember endless discussions and negotiations about that.

I have read that it was actually you who suggested to producer David Weisman that he should buy the rights to the *Lone Wolf* movies?

That is true, once we watched it together, I told him this was the one to get, especially since no one outside of Japanese audiences or a

Head-splitting gore!

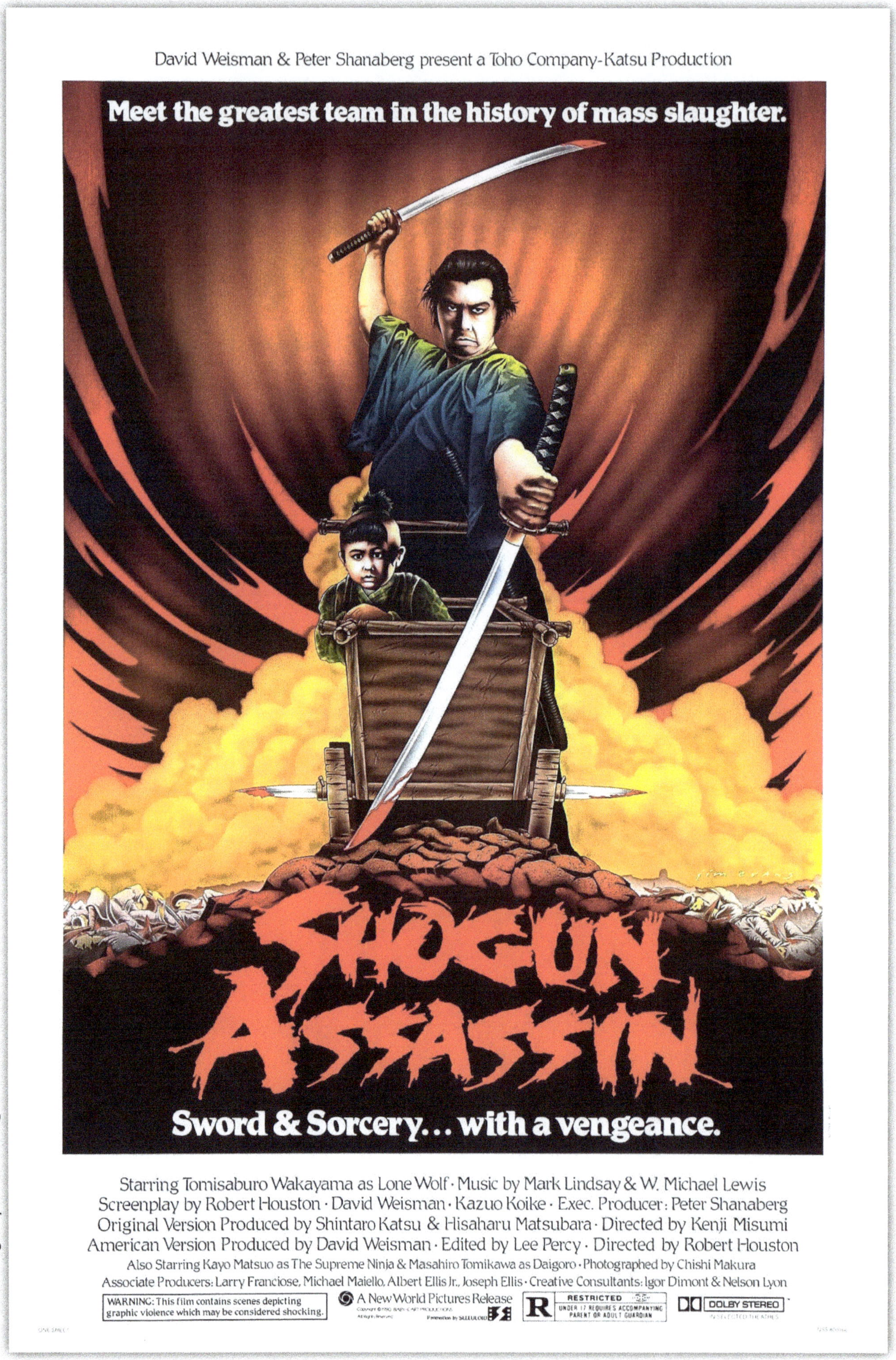

Jim's astounding US poster for *Shogun Assassin* (1980)

Jim's artwork is used for the UK quad poster for Shogun Assassin (1980)

Just the main figures from Jim's painting are used on this later Vipco rerelease DVD cover

few obsessives like me, had any clue it existed. Truthfully, I saw it as a revisionist western.

Your son Gibran provided the voice of Daigorō. Did you suggest to the producers that Gibran might be a good choice to provide the voice for Lone Wolf's child? His clear, quite sweet-sounding voice is certainly one of the most iconic elements of *Shogun Assassin*!

I was in a meeting with David and Bobby, and they were depressed that they had seemed to have exhausted every young actor voice they could find, with no luck. I told them I had a son with a tiny child voice, and they asked me to bring him in. They did a test and proclaimed immediately that they had their Daigorō.

Your artwork for the *Shogun Assassin* poster is iconic. How long did it take you to produce the illustration?

That illustration took about 3 weeks and ran right up against the print deadline. The army of dead ninjas in the background were done in a final all-night session at David's house, and we drove to the printer while the paint was still drying. An interesting bit of trivia is that Gary Panter, who was designing the *Pee-Wee's Playhouse* production, and had done the poster for Pee Wee, had also done a *Shogun Assassin* poster, but it was never used. Had I not finished on time, it would have been the one sheet instead.

What inspired the final image? And what art media did you use?

I really wanted it to look epic, so the background needed an apocalyptic feel, like a cathedral of blood. I wanted to try to bring Ittō's rhythmic double sword style to life and include his dead-eyed glower.

From a visual standpoint I wanted to show the danger of the baby cart, but at the same time make it look rickety, with Daigorō being the calm child, relaxed, but deadly.

Everything in the composition draws the eye to the two faces, standing at a bloody pinnacle in triumph, with a world of death behind them, their weapons tipped in blood. I used a combination of Dr. Martin dyes and acrylics painted with an airbrush, all the finish and detail work was done with colored pencils and tiny brushes. It was painted on illustration board.

Did you experiment with other layouts/compositions for the Shogun Assassin poster design?

No, with this one I sketched it out, David and Bobby loved it. I finished out the drawing, transferred it to illustration board, and painted it to finish without stopping or making any changes. The image in my mind was exactly what you see on the poster.

You also did the titles that appear in Shogun Assassin. What other stuff did you do for this movie?

I did the bloody logo that appears on the poster and in the title animation and got a friend of mine who was an Aikido instructor to create the sword slicing sound effects for the film by cutting through watermelons. Beyond that I just worked with David and Bobby on the editing and getting that epic soundtrack created by Mark Lindsay finished.

Logo designed by Jim

Have you considered re-releasing any of the original artwork that was created for Shogun Assassin?

I have considered releasing it in some kind of limited edition boxed set with detailed notes. It will likely happen, just haven't figured out what I want to do yet – maybe in conjunction with the release of a book or something.

Shogun Assassin has remained a cult favourite: it appeared as the 'sleepy time film' in Quentin Tarantino's *Kill Bill: Vol 2* (2004) and has been sampled in hip-hop music. GZA's *Liquid Swords* album (which boasts the talents of all the Wu-Tang Clan members) has samples from the film interspersed throughout it, which adds immeasurably to the tone and overall enjoyment of the album. **You must be pleased that Shogun Assassin, which you helped bring into the world, has continued to have currency within popular culture?**

My goal in choosing a career in commercial art over fine art was to create memorable cultural signposts. I felt that if I was successful, the world would be influenced by the images, and include them as part of an ongoing pop dialogue. With *Shogun Assassin*, my personal

obsession with Samurai films and Asian martial arts films helped launch a project that resonated in ways that I could never have anticipated. Being part of the creative team from inception to finish, I was able to influence all aspects of the graphics and production and collaborate in developing what has become an iconic pop culture milestone.

You started producing work under the moniker TAZ, and founded the TAZ collective. Many, many music posters have been designed and produced for leading bands and performers like Pearl Jam, Beck, Nirvana, Rage Against The Machine, Beastie Boys, Metallica, Foo Fighters, U2, Oasis, Porno For Pyros, Green Day and so on, plus

TAZ's art has appeared at many rock concerts and festivals

movie posters for the likes of *Jigsaw* and *Zombieland Double Tap*. Did you feel that there was more creative freedom for you as TAZ, rather than continuing simply as Jim Evans?

Yes, it allows me much greater freedom to experiment, rather than

sometimes leads me to new places in ways that limiting myself to being Jim Evans never would.

Jackie Chan is featured in a North American tour poster you did for the Beastie Boys. Have you seen and do you like Jackie Chan films, or were you just interested in using that specific image of Jackie Chan in that particular poster design?

I love Jackie Chan, as do the Beastie Boys. Together our favourite Jackie film was *Drunken Master*, thus that image was chosen. At the time, I was also working on the promotional

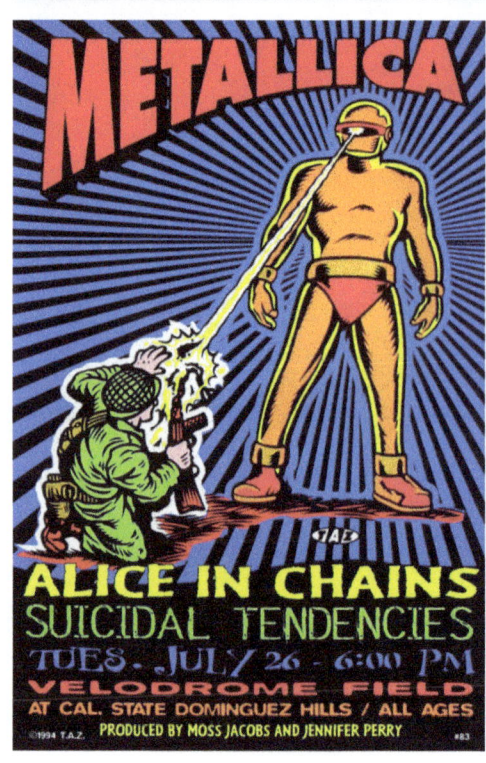

being tied to my own identity and the need to try and skew my output to just what Jim Evans does. TAZ was originally created to engage a new approach to doing rock posters, freely collaborating with other members of the team, and allowing them to make irreversible (by me) creative decisions. This immediately led to a more eclectic output, with aesthetically greater impact. Now it has taken on a life of its own, and materials for *Rumble in The Bronx*, and my wife Nancy and I got to meet Jackie Chan – a very charming man.

Did you create any tour posters for Nirvana?

I did not create a full tour poster for Nirvana, though they were included in shows that I did posters for. I had them headlining Lollapalooza 1994, but, of course, that never happened, so it got changed to The Smashing Pumpkins.

Most posters came from requests by managers, the band members themselves, or concert promoters like Goldenvoice.

Artwork collaboration between TAZ and RISK

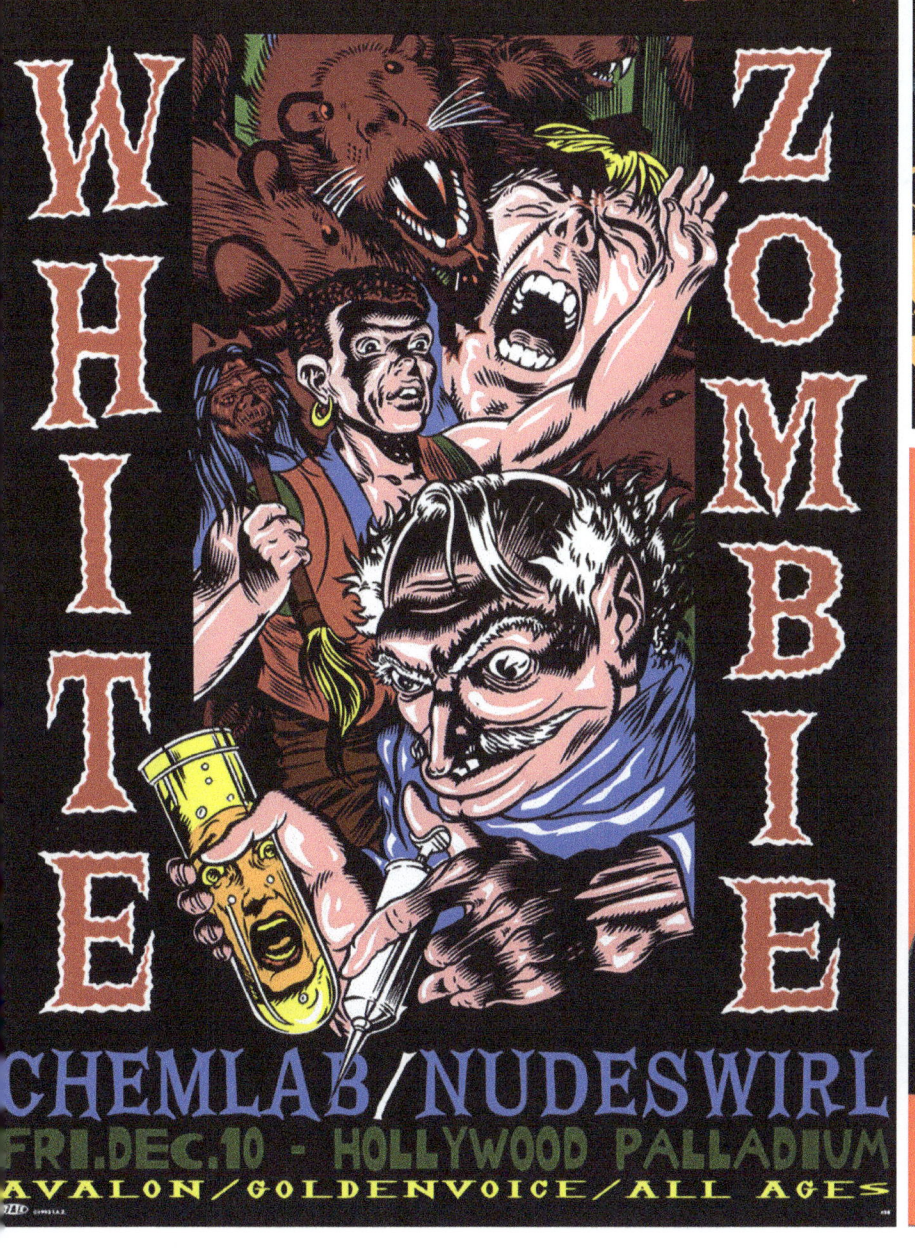

Page 69 Film Frenzy

Nowadays do you use computers to produce your art, or do you still physically create your illustrations?

I still do all my initial sketches and drawings by hand, as I still love to draw. The difference now is that I transfer all the drawings to the computer and use Adobe Illustrator & Photoshop for the final deliverable. It allows far more flexibility for change and fine-tuning.

Quentin Tarantino's *Once Upon A Time In Hollywood* (2019) famously recreated the LA/Hollywood milieu of the late 60s, drenching the big production in the pop culture of the time. You must've loved it when Sony Pictures commissioned you to deliver a series of portrait posters as part of the film's promotion. How did you come up with the final look for these posters?

I actually worked in Westwood during the Manson period, and was having breakfast with artist Ron Cobb at a restaurant only a few miles from the house when the news broke, so I understood the milieu quite well and was excited about getting that job. Tarantino wanted something that looked vaguely retro without being retro, and he wanted the image to tell a little story so they could be animated and easily translate to world-wide use for promotion. I chose two artists that were hot in 1969, Warhol and Rauschenberg, and combined their techniques and color usage along with my current graffiti influenced approach to fashion a unique set of portraits. The

The Legend of the Yokai

When *Teenage Mutant Ninja Turtles* (2014) was released, production house Paramount Pictures created an online exhibition, called 'The Legend of the Yokai', which showed work by international artists that explored 'the secret origins of the Ninja Turtles'. The Legend of the Yokai story was based on a folkloric tale of four Kappa (referred to as 'ancient turtle warriors') who vowed to protect a village from an evil warlord and an army of monsters. The show featured creative from 30 artists, including a very dynamic piece of work courtesy of Jim...

originals of the limited editions were given to the filmmakers, the stars, the production team, and the Sony marketing folks.

What are your plans for the future?

I'll likely be having a big art show at some point this year, and in addition to my usual poster commissions, various art projects, and limited-edition releases, I have some original properties I am developing with a team at CAA. One of these is titled *Sim Warriors*, and it involves a group of street savvy future-tech kids that operate in a not-so-distant future where simulation theory is a fact. I've created original art, characters, and intersecting parallel worlds where they battle an AI based adversary. Their foe is a next level up civilisation engaged in programming a multiverse of overlapping realities. It will likely initially be released as a book.

Thank you for all your time. Is there anything else you would like to add?

Yes, here is my *Eastern Heroes Film Frenzy* exclusive, that I do not believe has been revealed before concerning *Shogun Assassin*… At the time I was working on *Shogun Assassin*, I was also working on a body building poster with David Weisman that involved Arnold Schwarzenegger, who I had also met while working on a documentary with him. *Shogun Assassin* was almost done, and Arnold heard about it. He had just gotten the job to play *Conan the Barbarian*, that also included a surfing friend of mine, Gerry Lopez. Arnold asked if he could see a rough cut of *Shogun* to get some ideas for how to handle a big sword properly and add some cool Asian action to his approach. A screening was set up, and we all attended with Arnold. After the screening, Arnold was effusive with praise for what he had seen. When leaving the screening, Arnold, myself, and Gibran climbed into the elevator, Gibran looked up at Arnold and said "hi", Arnold looked down, pressed his hand on Gibran's head and said…

"Oh, so you are Daigorō!"

Jim's anecdote links these two awesome films together! Woot!

LIGHTNING DISCS OF DEATH!

Johnny Burnett

Lone Wolf and Cub Criterion Collection

Shogun Assassin FEATURE

Of all the incredible examples of Japanese cinema that have found their way to the West over the years, few films have had such an interesting and controversial journey as the awesome *Shogun Assassin*. Unjustly restricted from sale amid the awful 'Video Nasties' period overseen by the UK Board of Film Classification, the film broke free in the 90s to arrive uncut and in all it's glory, finally reaching us in Blu-ray format.

As mentioned elsewhere in this issue, *Shogun Assassin* rather skilfully combines two films from the exceptional *Lone Wolf and Cub* series into one movie, taking some initial elements from *Sword of Vengeance* and combining them alongside most of *Baby Cart at the River Styx*, adding the greatest voice-over in cinematic history to create a new film that is arguably more famous than the source movies it was so lovingly assembled from.

Thus was produced a new work of popular art...

Join me now on the road to hell, as I take a look at the various options you currently have available to you on shiny Blu-ray disc (or DVD, if that's your bag still) to own this slice of absolute chanbara heaven and, in a few cases, all the other movies from the series which gave birth to it.

Strap yourselves into the baby cart, get comfortable… and let's begin…

**Lone Wolf and Cub
Criterion Collection
Region A Blu-ray (US)
Region B Blu-ray (UK)
Region 1 DVD (US Only)**

Let's just cut to the chase and put the very best up front, in pole position: *The Lone Wolf and Cub* boxset from Criterion is one of the few samurai/chanbara releases from the label to be available in both the US and the UK. It remains THE absolute best restoration of the full series of all six movies in the series, and also includes the *Shogun Assassin* cut, so really it's a seven film set, all lovingly presented with gorgeous cover art and some really great extra features. If you only pick up one release from this list, make it this one. Hell, if you only pick up one single title from Criterion, make it this one. It's easily in my top five of their best releases of all time.

We get all six films lovingly presented from brand new 2K restorations, all featuring the original Japanese mono soundtracks as well as a new HD transfer of *Shogun Assassin*, the best it's ever looked anywhere imho.

Just look at these goodies…

> A newly-filmed (at the time) interview with Kazuo Koike, who is the original writer of the *Lone Wolf and Cub* manga series and was also the screenwriter on five of the *Lone Wolf and Cub* films.
> A cool 2005 documentary, called *Lame d'un père, l'âme d'un sabre*, about the making of the series.
> An interview with Sensei Yoshimitsu Katsuse, who talks about and demonstrates the real 'Suio-ryu' sword techniques that inspired the ones depicted in the manga and the movies.
> An interview with biographer Kazuma Nozawa. He discusses Kenji Misumi, director of four of the original six films (and is a favourite Japanese film-maker of mine.)
> A wonderful silent 1939 documentary that details the making

of samurai swords. This doc comes with an optional new ambient score by Ryan Francis.
> All the original trailers for all six movies.
> A gorgeous booklet that features film synopses and an essay by Japanese writer Patrick Macias. The stunning cover and booklet art is by renowned American comic book artist Paul Pope (who drew and wrote the comic mini-series *Batman: Year 100*).

To be blunt, if you pick any other release over this, you're choosing to pick up the ball and will join your mother in death, but if you pick this release, you're really, truly choosing the sword and can willingly join us all on the road to hell! It's absolutely flawless.

Available on DVD and Blu-ray in the USA and on Blu-ray here in the UK. These crop up fairly often on the secondhand market too, though why some folks choose to sell the set on is really beyond me. If you have the boxset already, make sure to check for the hidden physical 'easter egg' hidden inside the spine of the outer box: it's a fold-out blueprint of the baby cart. A one-off for Criterion who, to my knowledge, have never done anything like this on any other release.

Sublime: 10/10!

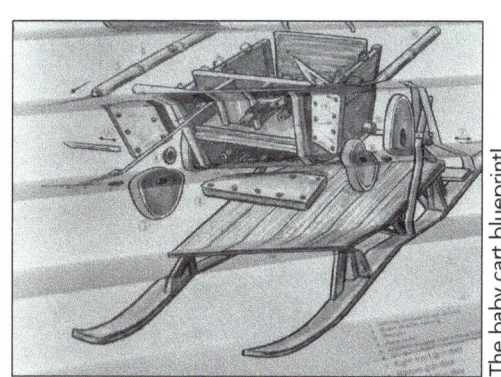

The baby cart blueprint!

Shogun Assassin
Eureka Entertainment
Region B Blu-ray (Region 2 DVD)
Out of Print

Maybe you couldn't care less about seeing *Shogun Assassin* in it's original form, maybe you're one of those curious souls who refuses to 'read a movie' and won't watch anything subtitled. You just want the recut, reassembled Western version of the material because you're a full-blooded *Shogun Assassin*-only kinda person (though if this is you, you're missing out on what is truly an amazing series of movies!) If the above describes you, then fear not my dear reader, as Eureka have you covered, or rather they did, because this is now out of print.

Eureka released two editions of *Shogun Assassin* as a standalone title: one version was a combo pack which contained both DVD and Blu-ray copies of the 1980 classic in a fancy steelbook, the other version was a Blu-ray-only edition. The extra features are very different compared to the Criterion release, and to some they will be of much more interest than the more Japanese-focused Criterion set. Here we get two commentary tracks, one with Ric Meyers and Steve Watson, which is ok, and is more of an amiable chat than an informative experience. The second track, though, is an absolute delight, as we have the producer of the US film version, David Weisman, joined by the original US poster artist, Jim Evans, and his son Gibran, who is the English voice of Daigorō. This track is so fantastic it's worth double-dipping on this release, even if you already have the stellar Criterion version.

As if that wasn't enough of a draw on its own, there is also a fantastic video interview with Samuel L. Jackson, speaking about his love for Japanese Cinema and for samurai movies in particular. This was filmed in 2009, when Jackson was firmly entrenched working on his *Afro Samurai* series. it's about 13 minutes long and is pretty good fun.

Eureka also opted to include all six of the original trailers for the *Lone Wolf and Cub* movies, as well as the original theatrical trailer for *Shogun Assassin*.

As previously mentioned, this is now out of print, but comes around quite often in the UK on the second hand market. Expect to pay about £20 for the standalone Blu-ray and £30-£40 for the steelbook. CEX is a good starting point for both.

Back in 2009 Eureka did also put out the original *Lone Wolf and Cub* series in full in a DVD boxset, along with an extra disc that housed *Shogun Assassin*. This set tends to sell for so much money these days that I wouldn't recommend tracking it down. The discs are all bare bones in terms of extras, and the quality of the transfers is nowhere near as good as later Blu-ray restorations. This will cost you far more than the formidable Criterion Blu-ray set (or it's DVD counterpart) by a long shot.

7.5/10 for the Blu-ray release
6/10 for the old DVD set (and that would be 5/10 if the movies weren't all so great!)

Shogun Assassin 5 Movie Collection
AnimEigo
Region A Blu-ray (US Only)

This is essentially the same *Shogun Assassin* cut and extras found on the Eureka Blu-ray release, but with the other 4 movies in the series (if we're counting *Shogun Assassin* as the first two) to create a five movie boxset. These 4 movies go by their alternate US titles, which is a bit confusing, but they are essentially the same movies, just with different names and they ONLY come with English audio tracks. This set

actually predates the Criterion release, as it came out in 2012. If you're expecting the same type of care and nuance in the audio dubs which was afforded *Shogun Assassin*, you will be sorely disappointed. I put this collection on the list for the sake of completion, but I can't in good conscience recommend the set to anyone other than those strange folks who flat out refuse to watch a movie with subtitles (which, if this is you, have a bloody word with yourself, mate: you're missing out on a whole lot of truly incredible cinema from around the world! Your brain is entirely capable of watching an image AND reading subtitles at the same time, I assure you!)

The set is, to my knowledge, still available stateside, though you'll obviously need a multi-region player to view the discs in the UK: they're all region A locked.

5/10 - Watching the English dubs of the rest of the series is a painful experience!

Shogun Assassin remains a curious anomaly where the recut, re-dubbed compilation of the first two movies stands as an entirely satisfying film experience in it's own right, and that voice-over has such a massive part to play in that.
It's really quite sad to watch the rest of the movies in English without it.

**Lone Wolf And Cub (Book)
Arrow Video
163 Pages**

Tom Mes wrote this in-depth, stunning examination of the *Lone Wolf And Cub* series for Arrow Video back in 2018. It's still in print and often available for just £5 in the Arrow sales, which seems to happen every few months. It's a truly wonderful book, my favourite of Tom Mes's many publications examining various periods and key figures in Japanese and Asian cinema.

It provides a amazing overview of the whole series, the stars and filmmakers behind the movies, the original manga source material, as well as all the various tributes, references and spin-offs that have come about over the years. The book gives a wonderful overview of not just the time period when the films themselves are set, but also the historical landscape of Japanese cinema at the time when the movies were made. Tom Mes is a legend, highly knowledgable and a far, far better writer than my clumsy efforts here to praise him can convey. Highly, highly recommended.

Oh, and also worth mentioning: the beautiful cover art for the book is by the insanely talented Kung Fu Bob O'Brien.

**The Bounty Hunter Trilogy
Radiance Films
Region Free Blu-ray (UK & US)
Releasing March 2024**

Lastly, for those who fall in love with lead actor Tomisaburo Wakayama (really, how could you not?!) and are keen to see more movies where he takes the lead role, Radiance Films have recently announced an upcoming boxset of the 3 *Bounty Hunter* movies he created just before he went on to make the *Lone Wolf And Cub* series. These are hella good fun, very James Bond inspired, with great soundtracks. I'm sure Radiance will put together a wonderful package for the boxset, which comes to the UK and US in March this year…

———

I've opted not to include the old, out of print DVD boxset of the full series that Eureka put out in the UK, or any of the other individual releases (on DVD or VHS) of the original *Lone Wolf And Cub* standalone movies, because that's a deep rabbit hole that will prove frustrating to jump into, as many of these can be very hard to track down and, anyway, are of most interest only to the real die-hard, gotta-catch-them-all collectors.

The *Lone Wolf and Cub* films look better than they ever have before on Blu-ray disc, are easily available stateside and here in the UK, and the glorious Criterion set remains permanently placed within my top five physical media releases of all time. It's a stunning boxset for a truly exceptional series of movies.

We can only hope that in the near future we also get a decent Blu-ray release of all five of the *Wicked Priest* series of movies, which Wakayama also headlined. They're as different from the *Lone Wolf And Cub* movies as his brother's bonkers *Hanzo The Razor* films are to Katsu's more well known *Zatoichi* series of films.

Whilst we're talking Zatoichi, it's worth also noting that Wakayama appeared in a couple of those films too, playing the brother of Zatoichi, alongside his real life brother, in the second feature, *The Tale of Zatoichi Continues* - and he returned to play an entirely unrelated character in the sixth feature, *Zatoichi and the Chest of Gold*. Criterion's *Zatoichi* boxset is a masterpiece of a release, but that's one for a different issue of *Film Frenzy*, if we ever get to turn our attention to Katsu's blind masseuse/master swordsman someday…

Thanks for joining me for this quick walk through Ogami Ittō's journey on Blu-ray, For more movie reviews, physical media unboxings, *Eastern Heroes* magazine showcases and much more Asian Cinema chat, you can find me still walking the path to hell over on Youtube…

www.youtube.com/c/thefanaticaldragon

He's not playing Ogami Ittō here, but Tomisaburo Wakayama is definitely always worth watching!

Hi, I am **Hector Martinez** and, first and foremost, I am a Bruce Lee fan. I've been a fan since 1966 when I first saw *The Green Hornet* television series. I grew up watching *Batman* and *Superman*, and when I saw Bruce Lee in *The Green Hornet* I became an instant fan and that fandom has lasted until today.

Back in 1973, growing up in New York City, I enjoyed watching spaghetti westerns and cops & robbers films, but when the kung fu storm happened, it revolutionised the way I saw movies at the cinema. Since 1973, when I got to see my first kung fu film, *Five Fingers of Death*, my main passion became kung fu.

I went to the cinemas every Saturday and must have seen all the kung fu films released from 1973 onwards, including *Deadly China Doll*, *Duel of the Iron Fist*, *The Chinese Professionals* and, of course, the Bruce Lee films.

In 1974 I remember sitting in the theatre and watching a very special, unique film that was very different from the hand-to-hand combat kung fu films that I saw prior and after. I'm talking about *Lightning Swords of Death*. I was mesmerised by Tomisaburo Wakayama and his little 'cub' Daigorō.

I loved the Japanese way of filming, the cinematography, the costumes, the colours and, most of all, the action... but I have to admit, I was shocked by the action! It was gory beyond gory! As with all things, you take it, tongue-in-cheek, and it

LIGHTNING SWORDS OF DEATH
ONE SHEET POSTER

Lone Wolf and Cub: Baby Cart to Hades was released theatrically by Toho in Japan in 1972. It was later released with an English-language dub by Columbia Pictures, titled *Lightning Swords of Death*, in 1974.

This American release used the poster tagline: "Raise a Kung-fu fist against Ogami... and he'll chop it off!"

SHOGUN ASSASSIN
ONE SHEET POSTER

This 27" x 41" one sheet poster for *Shogun Assassin* (1980) boasts striking, eye-catching art courtesy of Jim Evans.

The poster's top tagline highlighted the large amount of gory violence awaiting viewers: "Meet the greatest team in the history of mass slaughter." The second tagline seemed to be an attempt to tie-in the film with the early 80s wave of sword & sorcery films that were about to hit cinemas: "Sword & Sorcery... with a vengeance."

was enjoyable and, at the same time, still quite shocking! I became an instant fan of the *Lone Wolf and Cub* movie series, and enjoyed seeing Tomisaburo Wakayama, as the Shogun's decapitator, and his young son, Daigorō.

Then, in 1980, I got to see *Shogun Assassin*, which, of course, was a couple of the *Lone Wolf and Cub* films mixed into one feature film. I enjoyed that one immensely and I really appreciated the soundtrack. I own the US and Japanese versions

LONE WOLF AND CUB 7" SINGLE

This *Lone Wolf and Cub* 45 rpm stereo single was released in 1972 on the Toshiba Records label in Japan.

SHOGUN ASSASSIN SOUNDTRACK

This is the 180 gram "blood red" wax reissue. It was an official 2015 Record Store Day Release and was limited to 4000 copies.

BEST OF LONE WOLF AND CUB CD

The Best of Lone Wolf and Cub CD was released in 2004 in the USA on La-La Land Records.

LONE WOLF & CUB COLOURED VINYL LP

This was an unofficial release from the K.O. Records Production label.

The inner gatefold sleeve of the Record Store Day Release album sports a fine shot of Ogami Ittō clutching two blades, with Daigorō peering over his shoulder. This soundtrack album is definitely a shiny, gorgeous-looking piece of *Shogun Assassin* memorabilia!

of the score. Thank goodness today for Blu-ray, as I can watch these films repeatedly. I am also thankful to Criterion for releasing these movies. I also got to contact Gibran Evans through Facebook. We messaged and he was a great guy. I explained that not only was I a fan of *Shogun Assassin* as a whole, I also thought

A top view of the super-cool figures!

LONE WOLF AND CUB ACTION FIGURES

These action figures are modelled after Tomisaburo Wakayama as Ogami Ittō and Akihiro Tomikawa as his cub, Daigorō, who sits in his weaponised baby cart.

This set was part of the Alfrex 1/6 12" Jidaigeki Real Action Samurai Series.

Accessories include a cloth banner with calligraphy, the famous baby cart (called an 'Ubaguruma'), cloth clothing, and various weapons.

Come on, people, surely all you *Shogun Assassin* fans want an Ogami Ittō action figure, right?

LONE WOLF AND CUB BLU-RAY & DVD BOX SET

Criterion released this in 2016. It features all 6 titles from the original *Lone Wolf and Cub* film series.

that Daigorō was the coolest, cutest thing I've ever seen. I really enjoyed the English voice dub, and Gibran Evans was responsible for that dub. I sent him a photo of himself, as a child, and asked whether he could sign it for me, which he graciously did! Today that photo is in my collection, and shown here in this magazine.

I remain a huge fan of all the *Lone Wolf and Cub* films, which is a series that I never get tired of watching.

BEASTS FROM THE EAST

Carrying on from last issue of Film Frenzy, here are some more reviews of Chinese creature features! These films are unpretentious, fun, straightforward productions that make sure they never go on for too long and always ensure that their (sometimes dodgy CGI) monsters get enough screen time. So get ready to read about river beasts, gigantic wolves, rabid mutant tigers, fog creatures and tentacled terrors of the deep...

MUTANT TIGER (2022)

Starring Xie Miao, Hong Jianing, Xiang Hao, Zhang Haosen, Wang Yukai
Written by Yang Bingjia
Directed by Liu Wenpu
Beijing Bona Film & Television Culture Co.

The Great Eunuch orders the large-scale hunting of tigers after being informed that the big cats can be used to create Tiger Golden Elixir, which will increase his 'yang energy' (this elixir is extracted from tigers after they've been scorched with an ancient form of flamethrower!) Liang City, situated near the southwest border, behind Thousand Mile Tiger Ridge, is used as the HQ (referred to as the Eastern Depot) for this tiger hunting operation. But one of the captive tigers escapes, transmits 'plague' to the wild tiger population, and eventually the area is besieged by killer felines! Meanwhile, Zhang (Miao), new to the Imperial Guard, balks at being ordered to kill a rebel's daughter, and he takes out the other guards instead, in a snazzily-shot sword skirmish during a nighttime downpour. He then heads for the Eastern Depot to look for his brother Liuping, a tiger hunter, and soon finds himself caught up in the tiger attacks.

In due course Zhang discovers that the Eunuch's warlock has infected the tigers with a rabies-like distemper to create the Tiger Golden Elixir. These tigers, just like dogs with rabies, fear water, which Zhang intends to use to his advantage, to help save a group of survivors trapped in an inn.

The CGI tigers ain't all that, but the action in general, choreographed by action director Qin Pengfei, is good, and viewers are not shortchanged with regard to the amount of onscreen monster mayhem. Xie Miao, as Zhang, carries the movie with a committed performance, exuding a distinctive Ti Lung vibe throughout. This dude is pretty good.

There's a full-on tiger attack on the walled settlement of Liang City, with lots of folks falling victim to the scabrous beasts (every tiger in the world must be here, I reckon, based on the sheer number of striped felines shown in these scenes!) Though they're far from the best CGI critters ever committed to film, an occasional close-up of a tiger does look pretty sweet, with these killer cats possessing an semi-smirking expression on their faces.

Mutant Tiger is a decent period-set creatures-attack adventure romp that does kill off characters I was sure would survive, including three lacy robes-clad fighting femmes. In recent Chinese films you can never be certain if the hero will make it to the end, and here Zhang has a last stand on a rope bridge, which is a nicely handled sequence, showing him fighting off tigers and one of the imperial villains, who has swallowed the coveted Tiger Golden Elixir pill and has become a zombie-like, white-eyed, black-toothed, rabid dude who can command the cats! A mid-credits scene, however, does offer hope for Zhang's chances of surviving the tiger invasion.

CHANG'AN FOG MONSTER (2020)

Starring Luo Liqun, Cheng Qimeng, Li Bairong, Yang Ming
Directed by Lu Lei
Written by Chen Chong, Lu Lei
Produced by Runze Guo, Hui Qian

During the Tang Dynasty a mysterious fog envelopes the city of Chang'an... and within the mists lurks a gigantic Lovecraftian monstrosity, plus other, smaller beasts. The Crown Prince (Qimeng) and his loyal protector, Xiao (Liqun), who are walking the city streets at the time, escape the spike-tipped tentacles that start lunging from the foggy skies by hiding out in the Chang'an Guesthouse, where others are also trapped, including a stern swordswoman, an old hunter, and a courtesan. Some of the people within the guesthouse decide to sneak out to get weapons from a nearby blacksmith, and as they make their way along the deserted streets they can hear the grumbling, growling sounds of the mega-monster, noises that issue from all around them in the fog. But the group is assaulted by the mist monsters, the mission to the blacksmith is aborted, and the survivors are forced to continue to hunker down inside the guesthouse.

The plot includes a backstory concerning an ethnic group, referred to as Inhumans, who were blamed for an assassination attempt on the Emperor years ago, and are now seething with hate for the rulers. There are other characters who have varying views concerning the royal family too, both positive and negative, which the undercover Crown Prince finds fascinating.

Monster-wise, as well as the gargantuan central beast that looms above the streets, the movie includes lumpy-skinned, long-tailed, leopard-sized, reptile creatures that can eject organic spine-projectiles, and small, bat-winged critters with heads that can completely peel back, enabling them to envelope the faces of victims. The courtesan suffers such a fate, and she kills herself afterwards, rather than live with a ruined face.

Just like the later *Mutant Tiger* (2022), this production is another mainland Chinese period-set creature feature that offsets its nothing-special CGI with decent production values, a stoic, solid lead performance, and a simple but interesting horror-fantasy plot. There are some interesting touches here and there, such as the nicely-handled sequence showing the courtesan doing a dance performance, which prompts Xiao to recall walking through the city before the fog came, passing by characters who will end up trapped in the guesthouse with him. The film's quite brief running time still allows some space for a few dramatic showdowns, including the moment a vengeance-seeking Inhuman gangster releases a powerful incense designed to attract the ferocious foggy fiends to them, resulting, he hopes, in the Prince getting killed. When a boatman, a guesthouse attendant, and the steely swordswoman all die as they protect the Crown Prince from the attacking creatures, this deeply moves the Prince, and he vows to live on so that he can right all the wrongs of his royal predecessors and hopefully bring peace to the nation.

A detachment of golden-armoured royal warriors eventually arrive in the nick of time, dispensing stuff that, somehow, wards off the creatures. The humongous main monster, which has a bulky, blobby body held aloft by multiple tentacle-legs, retreats through the fog, away from the city.

This movie, also known as *Creature of the Mist*, is a contained monster-horror-fantasy yarn for the most part, set almost entirely inside the guesthouse, with the gigantic, spike-tentacled, mainly unseen boss beast treated both as a real threat and also as a kind of otherworldly symbol of the anger that has been inflamed by the perceived injustices perpetrated by those in power.

MONSTER OF THE DEEP (2023)

Starring He Zeming, Li Muyun, Zhang Boyu, Tian Haoning
Written by Guo Heawen
Directed by Wu Yingxiang
Tianjin Tmeng Galaxy Network Technology Co. Ltd

A giant, mutant, tentacled monstrosity attacks and sinks a ship in the pre-credits teaser scene, which is all well and good, but you do eventually realise that this beast is not the same creature featured in the rest of the movie!

The story proper begins by introducing us to Yang (Zeming), a single parent dad (just like the lead characters in 2022's *The Wolves* and 2023's *The Beast in the River*), who is haunted by memories of the car crash that killed his wife. To earn money to pay for his ill daughter's treatment, Yang agrees to use his explosives skills for a job that his brother-in-law Cui-Li (Boyu) recruits him for. Initially assuming he will be illegally catching fish using dynamite, Yang is far from happy upon discovering the job actually involves working with a criminal gang out to steal a very valuable diamond currently being transported on a cargo ship. In the meantime, a crew member on this cargo ship dies after a small octo-creature crawls down his throat and immediately becomes a larger cephalopod-beast, which goes on the offensive, assaulting other crew members.

When the robbers reach the ship they obviously find the place almost deserted, and are assailed by big tentacles that have mouthparts within the mouthparts! Two survivors are encountered - Mei (Muyun), a female employee of the diamond company (dressed in small denim shorts and white vest, which is attire that's popular in many of these Chinese creature features, it seems) - and Jun (Haoning), the son of the ship's (now-dead) captain. Yang's paternal instincts kick-in and he does his best to look after the scared kid, though this will mean dodging tentacles and dealing with the gang's obsessive need to get the diamond from a locked shipping container.

With its plot focusing on modern day pirate-type dudes boarding a deserted ship that's overrun with tentacles tipped with mouthparts, it's pretty obvious this movie is an unashamed *Deep Rising* (1998) knockoff. The story chugs along nicely, then takes an interesting turn when dozens of comatose victims are stumbled upon in the hold, with fleshy, flower-like monster-larvae poking from their upraised mouths. This is a novel, memorable concept, which the film does explore by showing Mei, who has a larvae inside her, developing a psychic link with the massive monster, resulting in Mei becoming aware of the creature's whereabouts at any given time (but it isn't explained why she doesn't slip into a coma-trance like the other larvae-infected victims).

Just like the raptors in *Jurassic Park* (1993), this monster is clever enough to open doors (with its tentacles), and Yang hypothesises that the creature could be the legendary kraken, but it is eventually disclosed that the beast is the result of lab experiments (aren't they always?) using a substance called Mutagen CZY-96.

Out of nowhere, whilst trapped in a container crate, Mei has an emotional moment, talking about her blind daughter, prompting Yang to reminisce about his own ill daughter, though the schmaltzy chat is cut short as the armed criminals burst back into the hold to shoot-up the *Quatermass*-like octo-beast. The film definitely attempts to remain entertaining throughout, with a profusion of scenes involving characters running around the ship's corridors, crawling through air vents, dodging tentacles, plus bickering and betrayals, and firefights with the swollen-headed critter.

He Zeming is okay as the do-gooder protagonist, who has some early scenes with his daughter that are rather too saccharine (but at least these moments provide some characterisation for the hero). Zhang Boyu, however, is far more interesting playing the amoral, money-focused Cui-Li.

With generally good effects, the film has Yang swimming into the massive mouth of the monster and killing himself by blowing up the critter with a bomb (does the Chinese Communist Party insist that these productions extol the virtues of heroic self-sacrifice?!), and the movie finishes on an open-ended note with Jun and Mei floating in a dingy in the ocean. Jun watches as Mei becomes possessed by the monster larvae that is still lurking inside her, but this rather interesting ending is immediately discarded when some hastily-added copy appears, informing us that Jun was rescued and returned to his mother, and Mei was nowhere to be found.

But, hell, *Monster of the Deep* is still a pretty engaging, tentacle-tastic *Deep Rising* rip-off that passes the time nicely.

THE WOLVES (2022)

Starring Ryan Kuo (Guo Jindong), Shi Zhenlong, Ma Yuan, Liu Yihan
Written by Rocky, Huang Siyuan, Qiu Junyang
Directed by Rocky, Huang Siyuan
Produced by Wu Yu, Kan Lun, Yu Yang, Rocky
Xiamen Gongli Film & television Co. Ltd/United Production Company

After a teaser opener showing a hunter falling prey to giant wolves in a cave, we cut to a group of characters on a passenger plane, which almost immediately crashes into a Siberian wilderness, and soon after the crash a big wolf makes an appearance: the filmmakers are not messing around with slow build-ups here!

These canine creatures have long, cat-like tails and lower jaws that can split in two (but this ability to super-widen the wolves' mouths is soon forgotten and not shown again in the movie). The survivors, including main hero Song Wu, his autistic daughter Jingwen, and Professor Ning, gather together in part of the wrecked plane's fuselage, making a fire to keep the critters at bay. Professor Ning is working on theories concerning mutant wolves and Song Wu happens to be a wolf expert: well, that's all quite convenient!

With firewood running out, everyone decides to trek across the snowy landscape (with the ropey, unrealistic CGI wolves sensibly kept mainly in the shadows), and the group reaches an area of trees where they're able to make new fires to scare away the vicious varmints.

Most scenes in *The Wolves* are shot in virtual environments, with several sets included too. This definitely gives the production an artificial feel, but it does all add to the heightened adventure style of the story, as characters negotiate sheer cliffs and narrow mountain ledges.

After a female character, Nana, cuts the rope attaching herself to the others in order to save them from being dragged to their deaths off the high craggy ledge (blimey, mainland Chinese films love a bit of self-sacrifice), the survivors encounter a tribal chief. This Siberian wiseman informs them that another expedition had come here years earlier, after which the giant wolves appeared...

Once the characters reach the remote tribal village there are some half-decent attempts at creating suspense, though showing a wolf creeping around a building, putting its paw on a person's shoulder like a sinister stalker, does edge matters closer to becoming silly rather than scary. But at least a modicum of tension is generated in these sequences, especially when Jingwen attempts to retrieve a walkie-talkie that has fallen outside of the hut.

When Jingwen is taken (in an offscreen incident) by the wolves, Song Wu heads over to the cavernous wolf den to save his daughter. Here he stumbles upon an illegal nuclear dumping site, which is, of course, the reason the wolves have mutated, leading to one of the critters becoming super-massive.

Song Wu manages to save a village child, but can't find Jingwen. So, after an overly-melodramatic crying scene triggered by the death of Song Wu's mate Bao, Song Wu prepares to go on a second mission back into the cave to retrieve Jingwen. As Song Wu smudges camo paint on his face, he muses that the giant wolves, which have become intelligent, decided to take Jingwen as a hostage so that they could draw all the humans to the cave-den to be killed. Song Wu marches stoically towards the cave, with his face no longer covered in camo makeup (?!), following a trail of bracelet beads left by his daughter. He moves deeper into the cavern to extract Jingwen, but knows he has only so much time before explosives are detonated to destroy the den. Father and daughter reunite and they succeed in reaching the cave entrance, but here they must take on the humongous boss wolf. Hey, but don't worry: Song Wu gets his hands on a batch of dynamite!

Though the filmmakers do attempt to infuse the finale with some heartfelt father-and-daughter bonding, the movie is more likely to be remembered for the poorly-rendered wolf monsters that, unfortunately, make this project a real dog.

CURSE OF THE KRAKEN (2020)

Starring Zhang Yuenan, Xun Sun, Charlene An
Written by Wang Jun
Directed by Wu Shile
Produced by Sun Lin
Xinghan Bainian Pictures

The film starts with a big, tentacled monster attacking folks on a beach, doing mean stuff like killing a newly-married groom. Then the story jumps forward and switches its focus to a ship, where a bearded captain is celebrating his birthday with his crew. Soon the monster arrives and we see that people become mutated, gill-man-style maniacs if the octo-beast rams its tentacle into their mouths

As the plot progresses, the protags find themselves taken prisoner on the pirate-run island of Gigitar, it is revealed that the ship's doctor is the widow of the groom we saw offed at the start of the film, and a tough female pirate, who'd earlier cold-bloodedly shot some of the crew members, now inexplicably becomes a 'nice' character. But the film's weak direction and acting means most viewers won't care about any of these story developments. And, to make things even less entertaining, the kraken goes missing for a huge chunk of the running time! All the action revolves around a single, marauding fish-faced mutant dude, who gets shot at a lot. Sub-par CGI beetle effects, mediocre melodramatics, a silly scene involving a flying, two-headed shark, and shoddy wirework all help to make this film even more rubbish! There's a cool moment where the kraken rolls along the ground in a novel manner, but then you remember that this is just a rip-off of the way the tentacled alien moved about in the fun flick *Grabbers* (2012).

A dockyard showdown is better that what came before, as characters are flung about and two victims get skewered on the same tentacle, but this is all too little, too late. Even when compared to Chinese creature features of a similar ilk, *Curse of the Kraken* is woefully substandard.

SNAKE 4: THE LOST WORLD (2023)

Starring Jampa Tseten, Chen Yusi, Zhang Haoran, Zhu Haijun
Written by Huang Lulu, Yin Chao, Li Jie
Directed by Lin Zhenzhao
Produced by Huang Lulu, Wu Jing, Chen Fenfa
Tmeng/Youku/Jiangsu Zhonglele film and Television Media Co. Ltd

A passenger plane crashes onto an uncharted island populated by killer vines, exploding fruit, lizard-monsters, giant toad-things and, of course, lots of humongous snakes. The survivors, including a man with suicidal urges, his ex-girlfriend and her partner, all trudge across the creature-infested terrain towards the smoking cockpit section of the wrecked plane, in search of a radio transmitter to call for help.

The yarn balances monster action and dramatics with some nice touches of humour, such as when two self-assured dudes address the crash survivors, telling them what they need to do to survive, only for both guys, in quick succession, to be killed off by the local vegetation!

The aforementioned flora consists of fruit with corrosive juices that can explode, and dangling, man-eating vines with giant Venus Flytrap-type toothy maws! The sequence that shows everyone desperately trying to escape these deadly Flytrap plants is most enjoyable.

After the vicious vines, the group stumbles across a region of narrow chasms inhabited by sizeable, iguana-like lizards with the ability to blend in with their surroundings, just like chameleons. There's a lot of action here, as folks get snagged by the lizard-creatures' long, pink tongues, which are tipped with fleshy appendages that can grip their prey. In this sequence, as in others, the central character is perfectly willing to attempt to sacrifice himself, but somehow he manages to survive the life-or-death situations.

Next up for all the survivors is a confrontation with a giant snake in some grassland. There are the usual scenes of characters being pursued by the CGI beast, until they are chased out of the grass and eventually set up camp for the night in a rocky area. Three of the group venture from their nighttime encampment to check out a light source, which they think might be a sign of rescue… but they realise that they've been drawn over to an awaiting toad-monster, which is equipped with a hanging, luminescent lure-appendage, similar to what you see on angler fish!

During the ensuing toad attack, the film actually manages to generate a feeling of sympathy for a victim, when we discover that his much-cherished suitcase is full of items belonging to his dead daughter, including a box of her ashes.

The lead protagonist, who seems tired of living and has suicidal tendencies and suicide-themed flashbacks, should really have come across as quite unlikeable, but

Jampa Tseten infuses his character with just enough world-weary nuance to keep him interesting. He gets placed in various sticky situations, where his willingness to put his life on the line ends up saving folks, whilst he is saved too, by those with him. Other characters are also thrown into similar scenarios and some are shown to be quite prepared to allow fellow survivors to fall into the beasts' clutches This all generates enough dramatic conflict to add some depth to the usual plot beats. Likeable characters get killed and a seemingly cowardly dude finds the guts to redeem himself during a set piece involving the plane wreck's jet engine, which is used to liquidize some of the huge snakes!

The CGI is generally really rather good in this film. The lizards, for instance, are matched well to their rocky environments and don't look 'added on', like less well rendered CGI critters often do in other Chinese monster-fests.

All in all, this is an agreeable monster island adventure tale that at least tries to add more dimension to its fatalistic main character.

JURASSIC REVIVAL (2022)

Starring Ma Xinyu, Feng Qilong, Yang Qiyu, Shen Yunzhong, Qiao Yaona
Written by Li Wei
Directed by Zhao Cong
Produced by Xu Yawei
Youku

This begins in the 1980s, on a newly-discovered island (the ghost island), where we see a T-Rex attack the researchers and guards at an encampment. Loads of bullets are fired at this T-Rex, but it keeps on attacking, and even dynamite does little to slow it down. One particular scientist is shown running about, clutching a dinosaur egg, and then the story skips to the present day (as stories often do in these flicks), and we're introduced to Zhao (Xinyu), the daughter of the guy-with-the-egg seen in the prologue. Zhao is asked by the despicable Mr Du (Qiyu) to accompany him and his team on a new mission to ghost island, the location of which he has rediscovered by comparing cloud formations on photographs taken at different times (a rip-off of an idea used in the 1976 version of *King Kong*). Against her better judgement, Zhao goes with Mr Du and his armed goons to the island. Other team members include Laka, a dreadlocked demolition expert, Sangji, a survival expert, and Yuzi, an attractive, stony-faced, gun-toting she-merc who likes to wear snug-fitting shorts.

Once on ghost island, a member of the group coughs-up blood and dies after a bug flies into his mouth, and then a super-big cobra goes on the offensive. The team are unable to kill the serpent with all their firepower, and are saved when a carnosaur rocks up and quickly bites the cobra in two!

An encounter with Velociraptors in an area of long grass happens next, and it is handled pretty well. There's even a decent-looking full scale raptor prop head used in this sequence, as well as a full-body raptor costume.

The characters eventually reach the island's open plains, which are populated by Stegosaurs, Triceratops, sauropods, pterosaurs, and other dinos. The quality of the special effects does vary throughout the film, with some of it looking particularly weak, such as a reddish-brown carnivore that is depicted here, moving about with a clunky, awkward gait. But the T-Rex that now shows up, with Zhao's wild-haired father riding on its back, is a better example of the CGI, boasting a more impactful body design and good skin texture details. It turns out that Zhao's dad has raised this T-Rex from the egg he was carrying about, and now the dino is his loyal pet. This is a fun, goofy idea, but the filmmakers waste the opportunity to show lots of dino-riding action, and simply have the dad tell the T-Rex to chill out while he joins the team, as Mr Du searches for a special meteorite.

The explorers reach a hot, volcanic landscape, dotted with jets of flame, which is the location of the meteorite. Mr Du wants to blow this hunk of rock up (presumably because it contains valuable minerals), but Zhao's father says that the meteorite's magnetic field is related to the life of the entire island, so if the rock gets destroyed every living thing on the isle will perish. So, after a raptor attack, the team members inevitably split into two factions, as some try to protect the meteorite, and others attempt to blow it up.

The orange-hued, fiery zone, where this finale takes place, is quite stylised and theatrical-looking, exuding a more fantastical, cinematic vibe (compared to the naturalistic locations used elsewhere), and it definitely suits the pulpy requirements of this lost world film. So it's a shame that it is used as the setting for a protracted hostage standoff situation, with Mr Du holding Zhao at knifepoint, which is all rather anticlimactic. We do get to see the pet T-Rex again, though, at the very end, as the survivors wait on the beach to be rescued.

As the film fades to black, some copy informs us that Laka, Zhao and Sangji were sentenced to six years in prison for breaking the local law: how the hell does a lost, prehistoric island happen to have its own local law?!

THE BEAST IN THE RIVER (2023)

Starring Lim Youwei, Hong Siyang, Wang Tingwen, He Jiangfeng, Gao Shaowei
Written by Wu Weijuan, Zhu Zifa
Directed by Zhang Wei
New Studios Pictures/Shandong Harmony Pictures/Anhui Mengyu Pictures

Single parent Gu Zhiyuan (Youwei) does low-paid dock work after leaving a life of crime, doing his best to raise his daughter Linglong (Tingwen). When a rampaging river monster comes ashore, causes havoc in the city of Tianjin, then abducts Linglong by snagging her with its tail (in a very similar way to what happens in the 2006 South Korean monster film *The Host*), Zhiyuan sets out to save his daughter. Aided by his journalist sister-in-law Xiaowei (Siyang) and a couple of his friends, Zhiyuan discovers that Wu Xun, a senior doctor at the local children's hospital, is the man responsible for creating the beast during experiments aimed, so he claims, at saving ill children's lives. Wu says that he will help them capture the creature, which is using the extensive sewer systems below the city as its lair...

Lots of action takes place within the labyrinthine sewers, as Zhiyuan, armed with a trident, slashes the creature and leads the enraged beast into a trap, where it is ensnared in a chain net. But Zhiyuan is immediately betrayed by Wu, who is in league with local mob kingpin Master Kun. Wu doesn't want the beast to be killed, which causes a rift with Master Kun, leading to a shootout in the sewers, enabling the creature to escape.

After some melodramatics following the death of his best pal, Zhiyuan is arrested on false charges by the Tianjin cops, but Xiaowei persuades the inept head policeman, Sheriff Hu, to let Zhiyuan walk free and hunt for the beast with his officers.

Zhiyuen and one of his buddies capture the creature in the sewers once more but, yet again, Wu intervenes, threatening to shoot the recently-saved Linglong if his beloved beast is hurt. The villainous Wu, you'll be glad to find out, does meet a fitting, fiery end, though the monster still roams free. It chases Zhiyuen and Linglong to the nearby river landing, where a cops-vs-beast confrontation occurs and grappling hooks are deployed to little effect, leaving it up to Zhiyuan to deal with the beast by ramming an explosive package beneath the critter's skin with his trident, resulting in a downbeat ending as the hero sacrifices his life to take down the monster. But, post-credits, we are shown Zhiyuen enjoying a meal with Linglong and Xiaowei, so he obviously did survive.

The monster in this direct-to-streaming movie, set during the Republic of China period, is a dark-skinned, toothy-faced, quadrupedal, long-tailed amphibious creature with a small-ish neural spine sail. The killer critter comes across as a kind of amalgamation of the fish-thing from *The Host* with a body structure akin to a Ray Harryhausen stop-motion creation, although the overall look has an alien creature vibe to it too. Though not in the same league as *The Host*, the CGI is passable, the action is brisk, the monster has a decent amount of screen time, and there's a final shot after the credits to set up a sequel, making this low budget flick an entertaining Chinese creature feature that's worth checking out.

MEG 2: THE TRENCH (2023)

Starring Jason Statham, Wu Jing, Shuya Sophia Cai, Cliff Curtis, Page Kennedy, Sergio Peris-Mencheta, Skyler Samuels
Written by Jon Hoeber, Erich Hoeber, Dean Georgaris
Directed by Ben Wheatley
Apelles Entertainment/China Media Capital/Flagship Entertainment Group/Gravity Pictures

What's this Jason Statham popcorn movie doing in the Beasts from the East section, I hear some of you ask? Well, *Meg 2* is a Chinese/American creature feature co-production, so let's read on…

Jonas Taylor (Statham), when he's not doing eco-warrior stuff like exposing illegal radioactive waste dumping, is a committed single parent dad (as many leads are in Chinese creature features like *The Wolves*, *Monster of the Deep* and *The Beast in the River*), who tells his daughter Meiying (Cai) that she can't go on the upcoming submersible exploration of the prehistoric world that exists at the bottom of the nearby deep sea trench. Meiying stows away on one of the two mini subs anyway, so Jonas must do his best to keep her alive after their submersibles are put out of action by explosions triggered by an illegal mining operation overseen by a villain called Montes (Peris-Mencheta).

Jonas, his brother-in-law Zhang (played in a no-nonsense manner by Wu Jing), Meiying and the other sub survivors must now leave their wrecked craft and trudge across the ocean floor to seek a means of escape within the mining operation's undersea base. This portion of the film is really enjoyable, with the scriptwriters throwing a lot of obstacles in the way of the characters, forcing them to exit their smashed-up subs after it's disclosed that their backup rescue sub has been sabotaged by unknown betrayers, leaving them with no option but to don reinforced diving suits and start walking through a bioluminescent zone in the hope that the brightness will hide their helmet beams from the enormous megalodons swimming above them. After encountering a toothy eel/lamprey and other denizens of the deep, they find themselves having to take a risky shortcut through a dark valley as their air runs perilously low. It's then a race against time to get inside the secret base before prehistoric sharks or some equally prehistoric, toothy amphibious beasties get them! Even inside this base the threats continue, as Jonas has to battle the vicious Montes, water starts pouring into the place, and a supposedly friendly workmate at HQ jettisons escape capsules before the protagonists can use them to get to the surface. At one point

Jonas even swims outside the base without a suit! One of the characters explains how it is possible for Jonas to do this (he has to expel all the air from his nostrils, etc), but I think the main reason Jonas can survive the powerful pressures at the bottom of the trench is because of one very important factor: he's played by hardman Jason fricking Statham!

As the story unfolds, Meg 2: The Trench presents us with giant prehistoric sharks and other critters escaping into the upper ocean after explosions cause a breach in the cold water barrier that usually seals off the undersea lost world. The movie also mixes in armed merc bad guys, a semi-trained captive megalodon, and underhand characters who're willing to kill their colleagues to cover up the fact they're running a rare minerals mining set-up in the trench.

Many critics and viewers have mercilessly ripped into this movie, but I think it's a really enjoyable, fun creature flick! Any movie that begins with a prologue set in the Cretaceous Period, showing a huge Tyrannosaurus Rex getting munched by a megalodon (okay, I know megalodons didn't exist during the age of the dinosaurs, but so what?), is obviously letting viewers know that they need to sit back and enjoy the monster antics coming up!

Director Ben Wheatley, better known for off-kilter, sometimes quirky, sometimes psychedelic low budget horror pics like *Kill List* (2011), *Sightseers* (2012), *A Field in England* (2013) and *In the Earth* (2021), here goes into full blockbuster mode, presenting us with a mega-enjoyable third act that sees the tourists at the holiday resort of Fun Island getting attacked by super-sized sharks, a huge octopus, and swarms of smaller amphibious predators! There's a fun shot seen from the inside of a megalodon's mouth as it chows down on hapless swimmers, and a gag where a tentacle disrupts a waterside wedding!

As the likeable main characters deal with gun-toting killers as well as the berserk beasts, lots are exciting (sometimes verging on silly) incidents are thrown at the screen: Statham hurling homemade spear-bombs at the monsters as he pilots a jet ski! A megalodon-vs-kraken fight! Undulating tentacles assaulting a helicopter! And, best of all, Statham using a broken helicopter rotor blade to skewer a megalodon through its open maw! Sweet!

Don't listen to the naysayers: just get a beer (or two), switch off your brain, and enjoy the on-screen antics! Colossal prehistoric sharks, a killer kraken, Statham being Statham, hordes of salamander monsters and generous doses of action: what's not to like?!

GIANT MONSTERS
POSTER GALLERY

Noriyoshi Ohrai illustrations
curated by Ken Miller

On the following pages are displayed a truly heavenly selection of movie posters illustrated by the late, great, uber-talented Japanese artist **Noriyoshi Ohrai**, who produced amazing artworks for science fiction movies, books and games, from the late 1960s up until the early 2000s. He is most famous for the stunning illustrations he created for Heisei and Millennium era Godzilla movie posters, the international poster for *The Empire Strikes Back*, and artwork for the *Metal Gear Solid* series of video games. Many of the Godzilla illustrations he did were for advance Godzilla movie posters.

***Godzilla vs. King Ghidorah* (1991)** Just look at this advance poster illustration by Noriyoshi Ohrai: Godzilla being constricted by his nemesis, the three-headed King Ghidorah! A nuclear submarine firing a big-ass missile at the behemoths! Godzilla stoically standing his ground, roaring like the king of the monsters he so definitely is!

***Miyazaki Art Center Poster* (2014)** A B2 poster used to advertise a Noriyoshi Ohrai exhibition that featured almost all of Ohrai's original art for movie posters, book covers, video games, plus editorial work, biology text books and more.

***The Return of Godzilla* (1984)** What a beauty! Noriyoshi created this simply sensational illustration for the advance poster for the first of the Heisei era Godzilla movies. So, so dynamic!

***Godzilla vs. Biollante* (1989)** What I love about this stunningly-painted advance poster is that Noriyoshi makes sure this works as a well-detailed depiction of the creatures, whilst also ensuing it is a very well-structured composition.

Ultraman Powered (1993) Dear god, this is a thing of monstrous beauty! This is a poster that Noriyoshi painted for the Japanese-American tokusatsu television series that's also known as *Ultraman: The Ultimate Hero*. I can't stop staring at this artwork!

Godzilla vs. Mothra (1992) This is Noriyoshi's dazzling painting for the fourth Godzilla film in the Heisei series, shown here without the poster typography. The decision to highlight the size of Mothra's wings helps to make this illo stand out.

Godzilla vs. Mechagodzilla II (1993) A marvellous mix of monsters and mecha! The titanic Mechagodzilla towers above Rodan and Godzilla in this Noriyoshi Ohrai illustration for the advance poster.

Godzilla vs. SpaceGodzilla (1994) This colourful, scrumptious illustration has Spacegodzilla looming majestically and menacingly upwards at the back of the composition. Honestly, this painting is so tasty it's good enough to eat!

***Godzilla vs. Destoroyah* (1995)** Noriyoshi makes sure that the image of the terminally overheating 'burning Godzilla' is centred in the painting, with Godzilla Junior positioned in front of him, hinting at what happens during the film's finale.

Godzilla vs. Megaguirus (2000) Another stunner from Noriyoshi, who captures the look of Godzilla's Millennium era facial features superbly. Red-eyed Megaguirus looks stonkingly amazing here too!

Miyazaki Art Center Poster (2014) Another B2 poster used to advertise a Noriyoshi Ohrai exhibition. This one shows multiple examples of his work, including an evocative depiction of Godzilla standing in a churning sea.

King Kong Lives (1986) Noriyoshi painted the Japanese poster for the American film *King Kong Lives* and really makes it look mouth-wateringly wonderful! This ace artwork definitely promises more than the movie is able to deliver!

***Godzilla: Final Wars* (1995)** This mad, mad movie is crammed with tons of monsters, plus lots of human and alien characters, so Noriyoshi does his best to include as many of the creatures and people within this montage as he can.

Tentacles (1977) I have a soft spot for this American-set Italian monster movie, which was one of the many creatures-run-amok films that came out after the success of *Jaws*. It's a pretty cheesy production, I gotta admit, and it is certainly not as epic as this Japanese poster makes it out to be, as painted by Noriyoshi!

The Visual Guide Book of First Godzilla (1983)
Noriyoshi Ohrai's sumptuously full-on artwork, which depicts Big G from the original *Godzilla* film, was published in *The Visual Guide Book of First Godzilla*. This Japanese tome was filled with examples of the 1954 movie's many film posters, plus lots of stills and also examples of the storyboard drawings created for the original kaiju flick.

Godzilla: Final Wars (1995) Finally, let's check out this eye-catching advance poster that boasts a dynamic rendering of Godzilla in a pose that shows off his magnificent back plates. What a handsome beast!

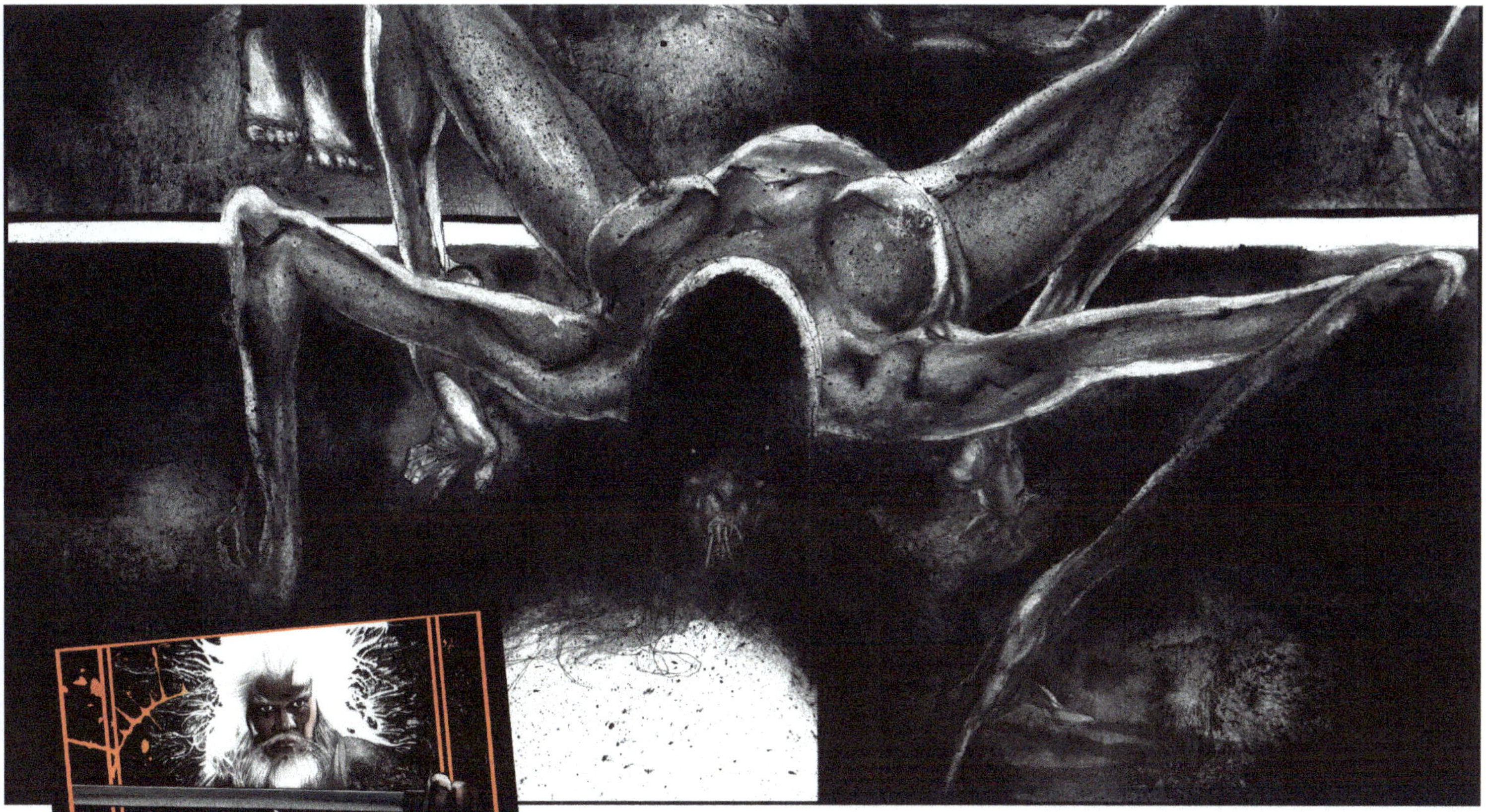

To purchase original art + prints by cover artist Russell Fox (Judge Dredd, Vampirella vs Purgatori, A Witch), commission storyboards + illustrations, and see more of his work, visit:

LONEFOXANDCUB.COM

ENTER THE CLONES OF BRUCE (2023)

*Starring Bruce Li, Bruce Le, Dragon Lee, Bruce Liang, Eric Tsang, Godfrey Ho, David Chiang
Directed by David Gregory
Produced by Andrew Furtado, Michael Worth, Jeremy Kai Ping Chueng, Vivian Sau Man Wong, Frank Djeng, Carl Daft, David Gregory
Severin Films*

In 1973, the martial arts world mourned the sudden loss of the legendary Bruce Lee. *Enter the Dragon*, which was his last completed film, became an iconic kung fu/action masterpiece, setting the stage for a new wave of cinema. *Enter the Dragon* was more than just a film, though, it was a phenomenon, and its impact was felt worldwide.

Not long after Bruce Lee's untimely passing, a unique genre emerged, aptly named 'Bruceploitation'. The first of these films, *The Dragon Story (aka Super Dragon, Bruce Lee: A Dragon Story* and *The Bruce Lee Story)*, hit the screens within a year, starring the appropriately named Bruce Li. As the world grappled with the void left by Lee, Hong Kong cinema exploded with imitators hoping to capture the essence of the martial arts legend.

Enter the Clones of Bruce, a fun documentary by David Gregory, delves into this intriguing sub-genre. Known for such captivating, splendid documentaries as *Texas Chain Saw Massacre: The Shocking Truth* (2000), *Lost Soul: The Doomed Journey of Richard Stanley's Island of Dr. Moreau* (2014), and *Ban the Sadist Videos!* (2005), Gregory once again tackles a fascinating topic. With *Enter the Clones of Bruce*, he secures interviews with the most popular Lee imitators of the era, including Bruce Li, Dragon Lee, Bruce Le, and Bruce Liang.

These interviews provide a riveting exploration into the minds of those who

Footage of Bruce Thai Bruce Le and Bruce Lai (Kwok Si-Chi) from the infamous Bruceploitation flick *The Clones of Bruce Lee* (1980) is, of course, featured in this pacy, enjoyable documentary!

Bruce Le is interviewed!

stepped into the shoes of the legendary Lee. Some reflect fondly on the experience, while others express embarrassment. The documentary nicely captures their stories, revealing the challenges and opportunities that shaped their careers.

Notable figures, such as cut-and-paste cult director Godfrey Ho, Bruce Lee's co-star Angela Mao, and 'The Black Dragon' Ron Van Clief, contribute their perspectives, adding depth to the narrative.

Enter the Clones of Bruce not only celebrates the legacy of Bruce Lee but also uncovers the motivations and the struggles of those who would become his cinematic doppelgängers. Gregory's documentary is a dynamic journey through a unique chapter in film history, shedding light on the phenomenon of Bruceploitation and the diverse stories that emerged from this intriguing period. ●

Bruce Liang!

Page 107 Film Frenzy